AN
INTRODUCTION
TO
HEGEL'S
METAPHYSICS

AN
INTRODUCTION
TO
HEGEL'S
METAPHYSICS

IVAN SOLL
Foreword by Walter Kaufmann

THE UNIVERSITY
OF CHICAGO PRESS
CHICAGO AND LONDON

ISBN: 0-226-76794-9 (clothbound)
0-226-76795-7 (paperbound)
Library of Congress Catalog Card Number: 75-85447

THE UNIVERSITY OF CHICAGO PRESS, CHICAGO 60637
The University of Chicago Press, Ltd., London

To Sandra, wife and midwife

CONTENTS

FOREWORD

This book is my intellectual grandchild. It has other ancestors, and I have other offspring, but I am proud of it without always agreeing with it. And, of course, it does not always agree with me.

The book's father, Ivan Soll, majored in philosophy at Princeton, and after a year's graduate work at Harvard and another year on a Fulbright at Munich he returned to Princeton for his doctorate. He wrote both his B.A. thesis (on Sartre) and his Ph.D. dissertation (on Hegel) with me, but by the time he completed the latter he was teaching at The University of Wisconsin—Hegel among other subjects. And since he got his degree he has done further work on Hegel, some of it in Paris where he spent a leave of absence.

Our approaches to Hegel are similar in many ways —above all, sympathetic and critical at the same time. But Soll deals with problems that are not discussed in comparable detail in my *Hegel*, and his orientation is less historical than mine.

My book aimed to show how Hegel and his philosophy were very different from the prevalent conceptions of the man and his system. Hegel's personality and development, the nature and aim of his *Phenomenology*, his *Logic*, and his system, and his attitude toward history were moved into the center. Balancing this concern with the whole phenomenon of Hegel, my commentary on the long preface to the *Phenomenology* involved some more microscopic work. My hope was to make a new beginning and to lay the foundations for further studies.

Good monographs on Hegel's aesthetics and his political philosophy, his philosophy of religion and his philosophy of nature are still sorely needed. Hegel's metaphysics is easily as important as any of these subjects, the more so because he has so often been seen as above all a metaphysician, if not the arch-metaphysician of all time. There is thus a special need for the present *Introduction*.

Soll's Hegel *is* a metaphysician, but not a proponent of the kind of metaphysics that was associated with his name during the heyday and in the wake of British Idealism. The Hegel encountered in the following pages is concerned with the relation of truth to human activity, with Kant's thing-in-itself, with subjectivity and objectivity, and with what Hegelians call the good and the bad infinite.

In one important respect this book stands in the tradition of Anglo-American Hegel scholarship. It is not an essay in the history of ideas, and there is little concern with influences or comparisons· Thus Royce's conception of Hegel's relation to pragmatism is criticized in these pages, but Dewey's debt to Hegel is not discussed. But anyone interested in that question is sure to find Soll's study extremely helpful.

In the second chapter, where Hegel's rejection of Kant's thing-in-itself is discussed, the treatment of the same problem by Fichte, Schelling, and Schopenhauer is not brought in. Soll's central aim, of which he never loses sight, is to show how Hegel dealt with some fundamental problems that continue to be of great interest to philosophers. In this way important questions are opened up in a fruitful manner that invites further reflection and research.

The style is exceptionally clear and straightforward, unencumbered both by Hegelian jargon and by current fads. Rarely have such metaphysical complexities been treated with such lucidity. This is a welcome departure from the tradition of paraphrasing obscure texts and, when the original becomes too dark for paraphrase, taking refuge in quotations. Thus this *Introduction* is a fine guide into Hegel's metaphysics and theory of knowledge.

The discussion of the celebrated section on master and slave in the *Phenomenology* is especially illuminating. It makes an important point that I had overlooked in my account, and after reading Soll's dissertation I therefore added a note to the Anchor Books paperback edition of my *Hegel* (1966, p. 137), citing him. (In the following pages I am still charged with having overlooked this point.)

The final section in this Introduction deals with "Passion in the *Logic*," with my conception of the dialectic as "the logic of passion," and with Royce's earlier use of the same phrase. As long as Soll has given so much attention to the provenance of this phrase, it would be stuffy to eschew further clarification.

The phrase "the logic of passion" came to me when I was a student, and it was with some disappointment that I encountered it in Royce a little latter, in 1942. While this was nothing like Scott's finding that Amundsen had reached the south pole a month before him, it was a fly in the ointment. Royce had used the phrase in an altogether different sense and had not applied it to Hegel. Hence I did not consider it necessary to mention Royce years later when I explained in *From Shakespeare to Existentialism*, at the end of the chapter on "The Young Hegel and Religion," in what sense "the dialectic of Hegel's *Phenomenology* is a *logic of passion*," and how "Hegel's own development illustrates the logic of passion." But in my *Hegel* I included some discussion of Royce's use of the phrase, leaning over backwards to be fair to him. Now Soll says that "Kaufmann fails to make clear that, when Royce uses the phrase . . . he does not use it to mean what Kaufmann does." Did I really lean over that far?

The final point in Soll's book is that I wrongly denied that the dialectic of Hegel's *Logic* is also a logic of passion. But it is only in the final paragraph of the book that Soll tries all too briefly in a few lines to persuade us of "the passion of the *Logic*." As usual, his point is worth thinking about because he calls attention to something interesting. For all that, the differences between the logic of the *Phenomenology* and that of the *Logic* remain remarkable, and the reader will have to decide for himself whether my way of putting the matter is really more misleading than Soll's.

Considering the traditional view of Hegel, it would have been a regression and some cause for disappointment if this *Introduction* denied the presence of passion in the *Phenomenology*. That the author moves in the opposite direction and insists on finding quite as much passion in the *Logic* comes as a rather delightful surprise. Most important, this is one of the very few books in English that will prove really helpful to students who are wrestling with Hegel's metaphysics.

WALTER KAUFMANN

PREFACE

"You see, at that time and in those portraits I felt that what I had to say was fairly hard to understand. It's like Hege' Hegel was a very interesting man, but there aren't many people who want to take the trouble to read him. He's up there where he is for the few people who want to give themselves that trouble and will go in search of whatever nourishment is there."

I told him these applications of Hegel were very impressive. How much of him had he read?

"None," he said. "I told you there weren't many people who wanted to take the trouble to go that far. And I don't either. I picked up my information on the subject from Kahnweiler."

From *Life with Picasso*,*
by Françoise Gilot and Carlton Lake

Hegel had a grand conception of philosophy. He conceived its task to be the attainment of a knowledge which is *absolute*, that is, without limitation. However, since some of his most important, immediate, philosophical predecessors had placed striking limitations upon man's cognitive capacities, Hegel had to rebut their restrictions in order to make his conception of the philosophical task tenable.

Hegel's heroic, if somewhat quixotic, attempt to restore the traditional grandeur of philosophic ambition, his reasoned rejection of that increasingly popular and powerful opposition to such ambition which had culminated in Immanuel Kant's *Critique of Pure*

Reason, is the central theme of this book. I believe that in Hegel's struggle to overcome the limitations placed upon human knowledge by his predecessors lies a major motivation of his philosophic method and a key to its comprehension. His struggles against the claims that man can have knowledge only of things as they appear to him, not as they are in themselves; that knowledge is only subjective, not objective; and that knowledge of the infinite or unconditioned is impossible, are traced in chapters 2, 3, and 4.

Regarding these issues, Hegel views Kant as his most formidable opponent, and Hegel's defense of absolute knowledge is, in large measure, directed against Kantian criticisms. Being primarily interested in the motivations of Hegel's method, I have not attempted to corroborate or criticize Hegel's interpretation of Kant, but have rested content with uncovering that interpretation and the nature of its influence on Hegel.

Hegel not only awarded philosophy the exalted task of attaining absolute knowledge, but also placed this philosophic task in an exalted position with respect to human endeavor in general. He presented the philosophic task of attaining absolute knowledge or truth as the ultimate task of all human endeavor; he thus presented philosophy as the ultimate form of all human activity. This general theory of human activity is traced in chapter 1.

I have focused upon three of the four books which Hegel actually wrote and published: the *Phenomenology of the Spirit,* the *Science of Logic* and the *Encyclopedia of the Philosophical Sciences.* The fourth, the *Philosophy of Right,* because it is restricted to social and political problems, is not as important for an investigation of Hegel's general conception of philosophy. These books form the core of Hegel's philosophy: they are more reliable than the many volumes compiled from students' notes of Hegel's lectures on the history of philosophy, the philosophy of history, aesthetics, and the philosophy of religion; they represent a more mature position than the *Jugendschriften* (which Hegel never even tried to publish) and his early articles in the *Critical Journal of Philosophy*.

Although I firmly adhere to the methodological principle that the texts which Hegel actually wrote and published are to be taken more seriously than the *Zusätze* (secondhand student reports of Hegel's verbal commentaries on these texts), I have made use of *Zusätze* where they clarify and do not contradict the texts actually written by Hegel.

Since I have sought to reveal the basic goals and concerns which motivate Hegel's philosophic exertions, I have paid special attention to his prefaces and introductions, for, not surprisingly, they contain the best statements of his initial problems and his general philosophic program.

It has become commonplace to contrast sharply the *Phenomenology* (1807) with Hegel's later writing in the *Science of Logic* (vol. 1, part 1, 1812; vol. 1, part 2, 1813; vol. 2, 1816) and the *Encyclopedia* (1817; rev. ed., 1827; 3rd rev. ed., 1830). And Hegel's admirers have often sworn allegiance to one while neglecting the other. On the Continent the general trend has been to study the *Phenomenology*, but to neglect the *Logic* and the *Encyclopedia*; in the English-speaking world this trend has been reversed. There are indeed differences between the *Phenomenology* and the later work, but I have stressed their often overlooked continuity and presented them as elements of a single philosophic enterprise.

Rather than following the complete detailed development of the *Phenomenology* or of the *Logic*, I have focused on certain sections in each which are crucial for understanding Hegel's overall conceptions of these works and his general philosophic program. This program, though ultimately unfulfilled and occasionally ignored by Hegel, supplies a useful framework for more complete and detailed studies of his individual works.

All translations of quotations from Hegel, unless otherwise noted, are my own. However, I have consulted and occasionally profited from Sir James Baillie's translation of the *Phenomenology*, Walter Kaufmann's superior translation of the Preface to the *Phenomenology*, W. H. Johnston and L. G. Struther's translation of the *Science of Logic*, and William Wallace's translation of the *Encyclopedia* version of the *Logic*. Where the original German text has been translated rather freely, or explains some stylistic oddity of my translation, or more clearly supports one of my interpretations, I have inserted it in brackets.

I have used as texts: Johannes Hoffmeister's 1952 edition of the *Phänomenologie des Geistes*, Georg Lasson's 1934 edition of the *Wissenschaft der Logik*, and Friedhelm Nicolin and Otto Pöggeler's 1959 edition of the *Enzyklopädie der philosophischen Wissenschaften im Grundriße* (1830). I have made reference to the page numbers in these editions, except in the case of the *Encyclopedia*—where I have referred instead to the short, numbered sections into which the body of the book is divided. As my text for the *Zusätze* to the *Encyclopedia*, which are not included in the Nicolin and Pöggeler edition, I have had to use the older *Jubiläumsausgabe* (1927–30) edited by Hermann Glockner. References are made to the number of the section and the *Zusatz* (e.g., *Enc.*, sec. 41, Z 2) . In general I have resorted to the *Jubiläumsausgabe* only where more recent and superior *Philosophische Bibliothek* editions did not exist or were unobtainable.

Paradoxically, the commentaries I have criticized most are the ones I have generally found to be best: Josiah Royce's *Lectures on Modern Idealism*, John N. Findlay's *Hegel: A Re-examination*, and Walter Kaufmann's *Hegel: Reinterpretation, Texts, and Commentary*. Interpretations which are neither plausible nor clear enough to consider seriously are not worth criticizing.

I want to thank Professor Walter Kaufmann, teacher, advisor and friend, who inspired, encouraged, and carefully criticized this study.

AN
INTRODUCTION
TO
HEGEL'S
METAPHYSICS

ABBREVIATIONS

The following nonstandardized abbreviations are used in the footnotes. For details, consult the Bibliography (page 153).

Enc.	Hegel's *Encyclopedia of the Philosophical Sciences*, 1830 ed.
Findlay	J. N. Findlay's *Hegel: A Re-examination.*
G	Glockner edition of Hegel's works, *Jubiläumsausgabe.*
Kaufmann	Walter Kaufmann's *Hegel: Reinterpretation, Texts, and Commentary.*
Logic	Hegel's *Science of Logic.*
PG	Hegel's *Phenomenology of the Spirit.*
Royce	Josiah Royce's *Lectures on Modern Idealism.*
Z	*Zusatz*

1 ~ PHILOSOPHY, TRUTH AND HUMAN ACTIVITY

Hegel's method is best approached by asking what he was trying to accomplish with it. Since his is a method for philosophy, it is naturally designed to achieve whatever it is that he thought philosophy seeks to achieve. What then does Hegel take to be the goal of philosophy? His answer in its most general form is as straightforward as it is unilluminating; the goal of philosophy is the truth. In 1817 Hegel dedicated the first edition of the *Encyclopedia of the Philosophical Sciences* to "this interest in knowing the truth."[1] Ten years later, in the preface to the second edition he still insists: "In general, that toward which I have worked and am still working in my philosophical endeavors is the scientific knowledge of the truth."[2] And in the introduction to the same work: "Philosophy shares, to be sure, its objects with religion. Both have the truth for their object."[3] In the *Science of Logic* the real interest of philosophy is equated with "the interest in what the true [das Wahre] . . . is."[4]

But this general statement of purpose does not seem to be exclusive enough; do not the natural sciences, mathematics, and even subscientific, unsystematic natural curiosity have truth for their object? Philosophy seems to share this object not only with religion. Yet Hegel would admit this expanded community of pur-

---

1. p. 22.
2. p. 3.
3. *Enc.* (see Abbreviations), sec. 1.
4. *Logic* (see Abbreviations), 1:51.

pose and even continue to expand it somewhat beyond the limits set for it by common sense and ordinary linguistic usage.

The magnificently ambitious, if quixotic and unfulfilled, program of the *Phenomenology of the Spirit* required ordering all the forms of consciousness (*die Gestalten des Bewußtseins*) in a single, ascending series, beginning with ordinary sense perception (*die sinnliche Gewißheit* and *die Wahrnehmung*) and working up to the philosophical consciousness which Hegel here terms "absolute knowledge" (*das absolute Wissen*). But also included in the series are such apparently nonepistemological and only partially epistemological forms as the master-servant relation, the conflict between human and divine law as exemplified in Sophocles' *Antigone*, the moral world view of Kant's ethics, and various forms of art and religion.

The book is remarkable in its scope. As Walter Kaufmann says: "To organize such a wealth of material—indeed, in a sense 'everything'—in the framework of one story is an astonishing feat."[5] No less remarkable is the limited means used to organize this wealth of material; the story is allowed but a single plot-line. The *Phenomenology* displays, however, not merely a linear succession of forms of consciousness but also a progression; the series ascends according to some more or less vague standard. Kaufmann suggests that the arrangement is made according to the relative maturity of the forms, and that "this does not mean that what comes later is always better and more attractive. Early childhood has its unsurpassable charm, youth in some respects is never

5. Kaufmann (see Abbreviations), p. 146.

eclipsed."[6] Yet this maturity cannot be equated simply with what comes later in time, for the development of the stages in the *Phenomenology* deviates radically from their order of appearance in history. But likewise, a person's maturity is not a direct function of his age. The process of maturation is not merely that of aging, and, although maturation does not imply improvement in every way, it suggests improvement in at least some ways.

The arrangement of the forms of consciousness included in the *Phenomenology* in a linear progression is of a piece with Hegel's view that, in some broad sense, they are all engaged in the same endeavor, but with varying degrees of success. Since the most mature or successful form of consciousness is philosophy or absolute knowledge, and the object and goal of philosophy is the truth, all the stages of the *Phenomenology* leading up to this form of consciousness can be considered as also seeking the truth but as being less adequate to the task.

But the notion of seeking the truth has a distinctly epistemological flavor, and it might seem that to view the *Phenomenology* in this way is to represent it as being merely an epistemological work. And certainly it is more. Although the first and last stages, sense perception and philosophy, are easily recognized to be epistemological, that is, as ways or modes of knowing, this is not true of some of the intervening stages already mentioned. If, like Josiah Royce, one were to approach the stages of the *Phenomenology* with a pair of putatively exclusive and exhaustive categories, with the be-

6. Ibid., p. 149.

lief that each stage, each form of consciousness, can be labeled either *theoretical* and *epistemological* on the one hand, or *practical* and *ethical* on the other, some stages would be classified as practical rather than theoretical, for they seem to be ways of acting in the world rather than ways of knowing the world.

However, Royce overstates this point when he claims that in the *Phenomenology* Hegel operates "rather by means of a reducing of the thinking process to pragmatic terms than by means of a false translation of real life into the abstract categories of logic."[7] It is just as one-sided to ignore the theoretical and epistemological aspect of the work as it is to ignore the practical. To ask which aspect is "reduced" to the other is unimportant, if not unanswerable. That Hegel denies any hard and fast distinction between epistemology and ethics, between theory and practice, between knowing and doing, is a crucial aspect of his philosophy. But this denial is not made by asserting either that all knowing is only a kind of doing or that all doing is only a kind of knowing. It is rather part of the following program: different ways of behaving are not to be compared merely with one another, nor are different ways of knowing to be compared merely with one another. We must make a more comprehensive comparison which also includes and reveals relationships between ways of knowing and ways of behaving, a more complete synthesis and systematization in which each way of relating to the world, each "form of consciousness," has its place in relation to each of the others.

In suggesting that all the stages of the *Phenome-*

7. Royce (see Abbreviations), p. 145.

nology are more or less adequate ways of seeking the truth I am not suggesting that these stages are merely epistemological. I want rather to stress that, for Hegel, not only does philosophy share its goal with religion (by his own admission) and with mathematics, the natural sciences, and ordinary curiosity (because of his too general formulation of philosophy's object as "the truth"), but that, as evidenced by the program and plan of the *Phenomenology*, sense perception, science, ethical codes, artistic activity, political behavior, and religion and philosophy are all considered different forms of the same endeavor. And given this vast community of aim and activity, the goal of philosophy is not merely the goal of philosophy alone but also the goal of all human activity. Moreover, this common activity tends to be described by Hegel in terms of seeking the truth, even where the particular form of consciousness considered is least obviously epistemological but rather prima facie pragmatic.

SELF-CONSCIOUSNESS

Both the fusing and relating of modes of acting and knowing, and the use of the quest for truth as the synoptic framework of all human activity are well illustrated in section B of the *Phenomenology*, titled "Self-Consciousness."[8] This is by far the best known and most influential part of the *Phenomenology*. It has been singled out for admiration by many, including Marx and, if imitation be a form of admiration, Sartre. Among the recent interpreters of Hegel to the English-speaking world, Findlay finds that the *Phenomenology* becomes

8. See Appendix.

"more lucid and illuminating" at this point and says that this section "has been *deservedly* admired"; while Kaufmann considers it the most interesting section next to the preface.

In the preceding section, "Consciousness," the first in the book, Hegel had treated three forms of consciousness which are all plainly epistemological.[9] The first, "sense-certainty" (*die sinnliche Gewißheit*), is, to quote Findlay's nice formulation, "the state of mind in which, in Russellian terms, we enjoy a direct acquaintance with some object which we *app*rehend without seeking either to *com*prehend or describe."[10] This object is not even the colored patch so popular with sense datum theorists, but is describable only as a *this, here, now*. The breakdown of this view, for reasons to be discussed later,[11] leads to the next form of consciousness, "Perception" (*Wahrnehmung*). Here the object of consciousness is no longer the directly presented particular of sense but the physical object, as Hegel puts it, "the thing" (*das Ding*). In turn, this view proves in-

---

9. Although only section A is titled "Consciousness," every stage in the entire *Phenomenology* is a form of consciousness (*Gestalt des Bewußtseins*). In the introduction to the *Science of Logic* Hegel says: "In the *Phenomenology of the Spirit* I have given an example of this method applied to a more concrete object, to consciousness." (1:35). And later in the *Logic* with reference to this passage: "It has been remarked in the introduction that the *Phenomenology of the Spirit* is the science of consciousness" (1:53). Similarly, the whole book is the *Phenomenology of the Spirit*, yet "Spirit" is also the title of section BB. An analogous use of one term to designate both whole and proper part occurs in the *Logic*; "being" (*Sein*) is the name of the first category, the generic name of the first three categories, and the name of the entire first third of the *Logic*.

10. Findlay (see Abbreviations) p. 88.

11. See Chap. 3, "Two Kinds of Universality."

adequate and is replaced by the "Understanding" (*Ver-stand*) , in which the objects of consciousness are not observable physical things but forces and laws, themselves unobservable but productive of the observable world, the explanatory constructs of physical theory. Consciousness then realizes that these unobservable forces and laws, these constructs of physical theory, are not only the objects but also the products of the understanding. Consciousness, in having had these constructs as its objects, had actually had itself for an object. With the realization of this fact, consciousness becomes self-consciousness.

Since the three stages of "Consciousness" are all plainly epistemological, neither the relating of knowing and acting nor the use of truth as the goal of all human endeavor can be demonstrated by them. Because the stages are epistemological, Hegel's tendency to describe the object of each of these forms of consciousness as "the truth" is neither remarkable nor illustrative of any supraepistemological, all-encompassing use of this idiom. And there is no relating of knowing and acting simply because there is no acting. If these two features of the *Phenomenology* are not demonstrated here, neither are they contradicted. The monolithically epistemological character of this section does, however, contradict Royce's assertion that in the *Phenomenology* "theoretical problems always appear as also life problems."[12]

In "Self-Consciousness," on the other hand, the plainly practical character of some of the stages makes possible the demonstration of these two points. Also manifest are the looseness of the argument (even

12. Royce, p. 152.

though Kaufmann rightly considers these transitions "among the most plausible in the whole book," and Findlay speaks of their "obscure but powerful 'logic' ") and the book's typically irregular structure.[13]

There is a general introductory section called "The Truth of Self-Certainty" followed by "A: Independence and Dependence of Self-Consciousness; Mastership and Servitude" and "B: Freedom of Self-Consciousness."

As the title of the introductory section suggests, the general characterization of self-consciousness is made in an epistemological idiom, that is, in terms of knowledge and truth. The previous stages of the *Phenomenology* are described as those in which "the truth is for consciousness something other than itself," and the dialectical process which revealed their inadequacy as that in which "the concept of this truth disappears."[14] Self-consciousness is then contrasted with its predecessor: "What did not come about in these earlier relationships will henceforth be the case, namely a certainty which is the same as its truth, for certainty is itself the object, and consciousness is itself the truth."[15]

Notice that in these quotations "the truth" of a form of consciousness is simply its object and is contrasted to the conscious subject rather than to falsity. However, "truth" is also used in contrast to falsity. In dialectically disappearing, "consciousness"—which takes its object to be external to itself—"shows itself rather not to be in

13. See Appendix
14. *PG* (see Abbreviations), p. 133.
15. Ibid.

the truth," whereas, "with self-consciousness we have thus entered the native domain of the truth."[16] To identify the objects of consciousness and self-consciousness as their "truths" is of a piece with characterizing each as a "form of knowledge" (*Gestalt des Wissens*). Both locutions are epistemological.

In self-consciousness the external world apprehended by consciousness does not completely vanish but merely loses its "otherness" (*Anderssein*), its character as an independent reality. It is recognized as being only an aspect (*Moment*) of self-consciousness, a product of abstraction unable to exist by itself. If the external world were not preserved as an aspect of self-consciousness, but completely annihilated and ignored, the resulting form of consciousness would produce only "the tautology, I am I."[17] This contentless self-contemplation would hardly be an advance, a more adequate way of knowing the truth. Since self-consciousness is supposed to be an advance over consciousness, Hegel denies that true self-consciousness can be achieved by completely blotting out the external world. The external sensible world must appear to self-consciousness, yet the "essence" or "truth" of self-consciousness is to remove any external object, to maintain its "unity with itself," to have only itself for an object. Paradoxically, the external world must be both preserved and destroyed.

Self-consciousness attempts to resolve this paradox by preserving this world but removing its external character. Self-consciousness attempts to do this by making

16. *PG*, p. 134.
17. Ibid.

the world its own, by taking possession of it. Thus, self-consciousness manifests itself as "desire" (*Begierde*).[18]

The epistemological quest for truth, with a sudden twist, expresses itself as desire, which, being the spring of all action, catapults the spirit from theory to practice. We take possession of things by using them for our own purposes. This entails changing them and *acting* upon them.

The action initiated by desire changes, uses, and possesses the external world but not merely for the benefits ordinarily associated with these activities. The immediate goals of desire and the behavior implementing it are viewed rather as manifestations of the basic drive of self-consciousness to negate the external world and have only itself for an object. In this respect Hegel's theory resembles other theories of behavior which view the vast variety of human activity as the varying expression of a single drive. Like Nietzsche's "will to power" and the "pleasure principles" of Mill and Freud, the desire of the self-conscious spirit to negate the external world furnishes the ultimate explanatory principle for a theory of all behavior. All the stages of self-consciousness are to be viewed as different attempts to negate or deny the reality of the external world.

It is the broadness of such concepts as *denial* and *negation* that enables Hegel to make the transition from theory to practice. If one is threatened by the apparition of a dragon, as the self-sufficiency of self-consciousness is threatened by the apparition (*Erscheinung*) of the external world, one may, without stirring, simply deny the reality of such apparitions. If, however, such appari-

18. *Begierde* has overtones of inordinateness, greed and carnal desire.

tions persist, as the external world continues to appear to self-consciousness, one may be tempted to slay the dragon by sword. Both the skeptical scholar and the swordsman can be said to "negate" the threat.

The transition to the practical realm is also aided in a similar fashion by the duality of the German word "*Selbstbewußtsein.*" As Walter Kaufmann points out: "While being self-conscious often means being unsure of oneself and embarrassed, *selbstbewußt sein* means just the opposite: being self-assured and proud. Of course, the primary meaning in both languages is the same: self-awareness. But while this sense is most important, the other connotations are relevant."[19] What Kaufmann calls the primary meaning is relied upon in the initial, epistemological characterization of self-consciousness; there the truth and essence of self-consciousness is to be aware only of itself. But when self-consciousness expresses itself as agent, the external world becomes not only a threat to its epistemological self-sufficiency but also a threat to the self-assurance and confidence of the agent. Also, "*die Gewißheit seiner selbst,*" *Self-Certainty*, is used both epistemologically and to mean self-assurance.

This negation of the world through action is still, interestingly enough, described in terms of truth: "Self-consciousness, certain of the nothingness of this other, sets this nothingness up as its *truth*, destroys the independent object and thereby achieves self-certainty, true certainty, as the certainty which has accrued to it in an objective manner."[20] It was previously noted that where

19. Kaufmann, pp. 152–53.
20. *PG*, p. 139.

a form of consciousness is discussed epistemologically, as a way of knowing, Hegel speaks of its object as its truth. In discussing a form of consciousness which is prima facie a way of acting, Hegel further extends the use of this idiom and speaks of its objective or goal as its *truth*. With this extension the notion of seeking the truth becomes flexible and imprecise enough to serve as a synoptic framework in which all forms of human activity can be placed.

But the negation of the world through action inspired by desire is doomed to failure. Even where action is successful and desire satisfied, the external world is not negated, for desire, though it may capture, use, and even physically destroy its objects, requires the presence of these objects for its expression and satisfaction. The satisfaction of desire reveals the dependence of desire on objects external to it.

Self-consciousness expresses itself as desire *in order* to do away with the external world, but instead, by requiring such a world to overcome, it insures the continued existence of such a world and, in turn, the continuance of desire.

This suggestion that desire inevitably contains the seeds of its own frustration has been taken up by Jean-Paul Sartre in his *Being and Nothingness*, a book heavily indebted to the *Phenomenology* and particularly to section B. However, unlike Hegel, Sartre attributes this fundamental futility not merely to a particular mode of human activity, but to all human endeavor. Accepting Hegel's thesis that the ultimate drive and motivation of human behavior is the urge to become completely self-sufficient, autonomous, independent of anything external by being both subject and object of consciousness, Sartre proceeds to argue that this is an unattainable goal, and man a "useless passion." Hegel, on the contrary, allows for the fulfillment of this drive but only after the spirit has endured the entire course of the *Phenomenology*. One might describe Sartre as a pessimistic Hegel, or Hegel as an optimistic Sartre.

Although the description of desire and its inevitable downfall seems to be made with reference to the external world in general, Hegel, in the course of this presentation, baldly asserts rather than argues that the object of desire is not the external world in general but that part of it which has life: ". . . the object of immediate desire is a living thing."[21] Findlay suggests that self-consciousness in the form of desire has "a more adequate exemplification of itself where a phenomenal object is living: a living thing has something of the perpetual direction toward self which is characteristic of the self-conscious subject and therefore serves to mirror the latter."[22] This gloss supplies somewhat of a justification for Hegel's assertion, but not one to be found in Hegel. To be sure, Hegel claims that the external object "has, like consciousness, gone back into itself" and "has become life through this reflection."[23] But there is no mention here of this external object serving as a mirror for self-consciousness.[24] Findlay glosses over the startling absence in the text of any justification for this claim, which is really made ad hoc, to introduce the

21. *PG*, p. 135.
22. Findlay, p. 94.
23. *PG*, p. 135.
24. Hegel does, however, use such an argument later in discussing the master-slave relationship.

discussion of certain types of interpersonal behavior which follows. To parody a phrase of Findlay's, the "logic" at this point is infinitely more obscure than powerful. It is the desire to include certain topics rather than any kind of "logic" which here dictates to the dialectic. And this pattern is not atypical.

To further set the scene for a discussion of interpersonal behavior Hegel makes the object of desire not just a living thing but another self-consciousness. Findlay again explains this move in terms of self-consciousness seeking an adequate mirror: ". . . the one clear outcome is that self-consciousness cannot be adequately mirrored in an object incapable of itself 'negating' what is external. . . . Another self is, in short, the only adequate mirror of my self-conscious self: the subject can only satisfactorily see itself when what it sees is another self-consciousness."[25] Unlike the previous move, this one is argued, but not in the way Findlay suggests. Desire is only truly satisfied by the negation of its object, and, since desire cannot bring this about through its own action on this object (as Hegel argued earlier), desire can be satisfied only if this object negates itself. Then, with extreme opacity this ability to negate is identified with self-consciousness, and Hegel concludes: "Self-consciousness achieves satisfaction only in another self-consciousness."[26]

Findlay's interpretation is too epistemological. If one were to describe the attainment of life and self-consciousness by the object of self-consciousness in terms of his mirror metaphor, it would be well to remember

25. Findlay, p. 94.
26. PG, p. 139.

that self-consciousness is here expressing itself as the desire to destroy through action. What self-consciousness seeks in the hall of mirrors is not an accurate image of itself to contemplate but a flawed pane whose destructibility affords an escape route to independence.

After generally delineating the basic drive of self-consciousness as the attempt to achieve self-sufficiency by negating everything external to itself, Hegel exemplifies this drive in a variety of more specific forms.

THE LIFE AND DEATH STRUGGLE

As the result of the preceding development, "the other is also a self-consciousness; individual confronts individual."[27] We are now in the social sphere, but in an antisocial way. Each of these individual self-consciousnesses tries to negate the other by killing it and must risk its own life to do so. They engage in a "life and death struggle" which is the direct consequence of the general character of each self-consciousness to negate whatever is external to it.

But by referring to the realization of the drive toward self-sufficiency and self-certainty as its *truth*, even this struggle is discussed as a kind of seeking after truth: "They must enter this struggle, for they must lift their self-certainty to the *truth*. . . . The individual who has not risked his life can, of course, be recognized as a *person*, but he has not achieved the *truth* of this recognition as an independent self-consciousness."[28] Even where least expected, the goal remains "the truth."

The reasons for the failure of this attempt to achieve

27. *PG*, p. 143.
28. *PG*, p. 144.

true self-consciousness through the death of the other and the transition to the next stage are only obscurely indicated by Hegel. Kaufmann suggests that the life and death struggle gives way to the master-slave relationship because "the loser prefers servitude to death."[29] But why should the winner bent upon the death of the other allow his victim this option? Findlay is vague on this question: "To carry on this struggle till it results in the death of one of the parties will, however, remove a necessary condition of self-consciousness."[30] Although Findlay never tells us what this condition is, his suggestion that the struggle is abandoned because the murdering *winner* finds his victory somehow unsatisfactory seems sound.

Royce attributes this unsatisfactoriness to "the fact that killing a man proves nothing, except the victor, in order to prove himself to be the self, needs still another man to kill."[31] Royce's explanation of this transition is essentially an application of Hegel's argument for the inevitable frustration of desire in general.[32] And although it is applicable, there is no textual evidence that Hegel actually invokes this argument here.

As I have tried to show, Hegel arrives at the conclusion that self-consciousness must have another self-consciousness as its object, not by stressing its epistemological need for an adequate mirror, but by stressing its need to negate the external world. However, in making the transition from the life and death struggle to the master-servant relationship, Hegel uses this con-

29. Kaufmann, p. 153.
30. Findlay, p. 96.
. 31. Royce, p. 177.
32. See Chap. 1, "Self-consciousness."

clusion by giving it an epistemological twist. Suddenly,
at the very beginning of section IV A, the second self-
consciousness is asserted to be necessary for the assurance and autonomy of the first, not because it can be
destroyed, but because this assurance and autonomy
require a *witness*: "Self-consciousness exists in itself
and for itself because it exists as such for another self-
consciousness, that is, it exists only by being recognized."[33] The other suddenly becomes, not a threat
and obstacle to self-realization, necessary only as something to destroy, but an accomplice to be preserved.
"Each is the other's *means* (*Mittel*) through which it
mediates (*vermittelt*) and unites with itself, and each
. . . exists for itself only through this mediation (*Ver-
mittlung*) . They recognize themselves as mutually recognizing each other."[34] The need for a witness, though
itself merely postulated and not justified, enables Hegel
to make this transition.

The other has now been deemed necessary both because of its vulnerability and its awareness; self-consciousness requires both a mortal enemy to destroy and
a witness to whom it can demonstrate its willingness to
risk its life in mortal combat. But where the enemy is
the only witness, victory insures lack of recognition.
And since victory is meaningful only when recognized
by another, victory becomes impossible. Hegel speaks
of death as the "natural negation of life . . . which remains without the required significance of recognition."[35] Since killing the enemy also destroys the

33. *PG*, p. 141.
34. *PG*, p. 143.
35. *PG*, p. 145.

witness, a way must be found to negate the other while preserving his ability to witness. So the victor makes the vanquished his vassal instead of his victim.

It is not, as Kaufmann claims, that the loser prefers servitude to death, but rather that the winner prefers a servant to a corpse. And the assurance of even the successful head hunter is flawed not, as Royce claims, just because "even head hunting implies dependence upon one's neighbor who is good enough to furnish one more head for the hunter,"[36] but also because the successful head hunter's potential admiring public is constantly shrinking.

MASTER AND SERVANT

The two self-consciousnesses are now related as master and servant. This relation is the result of attempts by self-consciousness to achieve two sometimes conflicting goals, the negation of everything external to it, and recognition. It seems at first that the master has solved both of these problems. Since desire requires external objects for its satisfaction, it cannot successfully negate the external world. The servant, as a self-consciousness, tries to negate the external world by changing it through work, but although work can change the world, it cannot completely negate or destroy it. For him the world is an autonomous entity with which he must cope. But the master, by setting the servant to work for him, derives "enjoyment" from this world without having to cope with it, without having to experience its "autonomy" (Selbständigkeit). Thus, he succeeds where desire failed, negates the external world, and becomes "the

36. Royce, p. 177.

purely negative power for which the thing is nothing."
The servant also furnishes him with the recognition required by self-consciousness.

Then, in a sharp reversal, which deeply influenced
Karl Marx, the servant emerges as the higher realization
of self-consciousness. There are three arguments offered
for this conclusion. First, since each serves as the object
or "truth" of the other, the inferior one (the servant)
has the superior one (the master) for an object and thus
has a higher truth: "For the master the inessential consciousness is the object which constitutes the truth of
his self-certainty. . . . For servitude the essence is the
master; thus its truth is the independent consciousness
existing for itself."[37]

This is outrageous; one might analogously argue that
the loser of a chess game knew more about chess than
the winner because the loser could observe the superior
play of the winner, while the winner could observe only
the inferior play of the loser.

Secondly, since the servant "felt the fear of death,
the absolute master," and, because of it, "trembled
throughout, making all that was stable in him shudder,"
he has the independent consciousness not only for his
object but also *in himself*, because, "this pure universal
movement [the trembling], the absolute dissolving of all
that is enduring [the shuddering], is however the simple
essence of self-consciousness."[38] This is certainly more
poetically impressionistic than philosophically impressive, more of a metaphor than an argument.

37. PG, pp. 147–48. Findlay's misplaced mirror metaphor seems to
fit this passage better than the ones to which it is applied.
38. PG, p. 148.

Thirdly, although the enjoyment of the master is a "pure negation of the object," which produces "unalloyed self-reliance, [Selbstgefühl]," Hegel argues: "This satisfaction is, for that very reason, itself only evanescent, for it lacks the *objective* side or *continued existence* [Bestehen]. Work, on the contrary, is restrained desire, arrested evanescence; work, in other words, shapes and forms [bildet]."[39] The fleeting enjoyments of the master do not last, but the servant, because he does not and cannot completely negate the objects he works on, creates something enduring (*ein Bleibendes*).

The downfall of desire was its failure to do away with external objects, but now this same failure is cited as responsible for the success of the servant. Does not the continued existence of the external object limit the practical independence and epistemological autonomy of the servant, just as it limited desire? It does not, for the servant having given form to the object by working on it, recognizes himself in the object and thus removes its external character.

One extremely plausible interpretation of the ascendancy of the servant, and one attractive to Marxists, is also offered by Kaufmann: "The servant comes to live by his own work and thus becomes self-reliant and independent, while the master comes to rely on the servant's labor and thus becomes dependent."[40] And Royce says, "Unfortunately, however, for the master, the master becomes dependent upon the slave's work."[41] But as

39. *PG*, pp. 148–49.
40. Kaufmann, p. 153.
41. Royce, p. 178.

sensible as this way to argue the superiority of the servant would have been, Hegel himself does not, in fact, use it.

The ensuing transition from the master-servant relationship to the next form of consciousness, *stoicism*, is again inadequately described by the commentators. Findlay's interpretation is: "The slave's labour is also a more genuine overcoming of material externality than the master's idle round of vanishing enjoyments. But, since for the slave all rational direction lies outside himself in the master, his self-assertion will be necessarily degraded to self-will *(Eigensinn)*, and his intelligence to a relatively hidebound skill or aptitude *(Geschicklichkeit)*. It is only in an attitude that can rise *above* the whole master-slave distinction that self-consciousness can be adequately realized."[42] The passage to which Findlay refers[43] is not even relevant and must be strangely read to make it yield an explanation of a transition it does not discuss. The passage occurs immediately after the servant discovers himself in the products of his work. Hegel nowhere says that this "rediscovery of its own mind and significance *(seinen eigenen Sinn)* in work" is necessarily degraded to mere capricious obstinacy *(Eigensinn)*[44] and skill because this work is externally directed by the master. Findlay's gloss is suspiciously incoherent and paradoxical; should not the master's external direction prevent all caprice and obstinacy on the part of the servant rather than produce it?

42. Findlay, p. 96.
43. The last paragraph in IV. A, pp. 149–50.
44. *Sinn* means both mind and significance; *Eigensinn* means both caprice and obstinacy; all these meanings are relevant.

Hegel actually argues only that unless the work and rediscovery are accompanied by absolute fear, this degradation occurs: "If consciousness forms without the prime absolute fear, it is only its own mind and significance in a vain way."[45] But as was plainly stated in Hegel's second argument for the ascendancy of the servant, the servant does experience absolute fear.[46] Hegel is not describing the servant's inevitable failure, but one of the necessary conditions of his actual success. No transition is being discussed here.

Moreover, the fact that the servant obeys orders, the very fact which Findlay claims to be responsible for the servant's failure, is here cited as another necessary condition for his success: "For this reflection [self-discovery] both the elements [*Momente*] of fear and *service* in general, like that of giving form, are necessary. . . . Without the discipline of service and obedience, fear remains formal and does not spread itself over the known actuality of existence."[47]

Both Kaufmann and Royce view the transition to stoicism as occurring simply with the servant's *recognition* of his own superiority and independence. Kaufmann says, "The transition to the first of these outlooks is easy to follow: the attitude of the servant who, despite his status, feels essentially self-reliant and independent may be characterized as stoicism."[48] Royce says, "Let this essential character of the slave,—the fact that he, as worker, is the only true man in this primitive society —let this fact come to his own consciousness, and the

45. *PG*, p. 150.
46. See above.
47. *PG*, p. 149.
48. Kaufmann, p. 153.

self becomes transformed from slavery to a higher phase of consciousness. This new phase is represented . . . by stoicism."[49]

But Hegel gives reasons for the *inadequacy* of the servant's independence and autonomy, even where they are recognized by the servant. In this transition the servant's independence is not merely recognized but also rejected and replaced. In short, there is more of a transition than Royce or Kaufmann indicate.

The basic drive of self-consciousness is to become its own object, to collapse the distinction between consciousness and its object. The servant's failure to complete this unification is the inadequacy which initiates the transition. The servant's self-consciousness recognizes itself in two ways—in the master and in the objects it works on. In each it sees itself; in the master, it sees itself as a consciousness; in the artifact, it sees itself objectified in the form it imparts to the *object*. "The repressed self-consciousness [the servant], in the activity of forming, becomes its own object [in the sense that it is embodied] in the form of the fashioned object. At the same time it sees in the master being for itself [*Fürsichsein*, here roughly synonymous with self-consciousness] as a consciousness."[50] But for the servant, the master and the artifacts, that is, consciousness and object, are separate and distinct: "But in the servant's consciousness as such, these two elements, itself as an independent object and this object as a consciousness, fall asunder and thus its own essence falls asunder."[51]

49. Royce, p. 178.
50. *PG*, p. 151.
51. Ibid.

Where consciousness is not identical with its object, there is no true *self*-consciousness. Although the servant cannot know it, "the thinghood which the form receives through work is nothing other than [*keine andere Substanz als*] consciousness."[52] A transition must be made to a new form of consciousness which is able to recognize and thus bring about this identity between subject and object.

The servant recognizing himself in his artifacts approaches this identity, but to the extent that he still admits the separation of artisan and artifact, of consciousness and object, he falls short.

STOICISM

Stoicism is viewed as a denial of the external world and correspondingly of the subject-object distinction. This denial is accomplished by withdrawing from the life of action, from the servant's attempt to effect the external world by acting on it, to a life of *thought*. Action, be it the crude destruction of desire and war or the constructive creation of work, never succeeds in doing away with the need for an external object and thus with the subject-object distinction.

Action was originally resorted to by the self-conscious spirit when mere contemplation failed to accomplish this very task.[53] Now it seems that with the failure of action, the spirit in desperation hopelessly *reverts* to contemplation. But this is not so.

The transition from action to thought is not merely

52. Ibid.
53. See Chap. 1, "Self-consciousness."

a return from action to contemplation in general. *Thought (Denken)* is distinguished from other ways of knowing the world, in particular from knowing by means of sense perception, and thus from the stages in Section A, "Consciousness": "The object comes to thought not in sensible representations or figures [*in Vorstellungen oder Gestalten*] but in concepts [*Begriffen*] . . ."⁵⁴

Unlike sense-certainty, perception, and understanding, thought is not an attempt to know an external world. When one thinks concepts, no reference is made to anything external. For concepts are not only objects of the thinking consciousness but also its products. Furthermore, the fact that concepts belong to the thinking consciousness and are not external to it is immediately obvious: "What is represented sensuously, as existing and having a shape, has as such the form of being something other than consciousness; but a concept . . . is not like a representation, where one has first to recollect that it is one's own representation, but the concept is for me immediately *my* concept."⁵⁵ Hegel is arguing that the mental images produced by perception of the external world and by sensuous imagination are similar. When one entertains such an image, one must ask oneself whether it is one's own product or that of the external world, whether it is imagination or perception. But when one considers an abstract, non-sensuous concept, there is no comparable alternative. If it is a concept, it must have been produced by me. Thus the

54. *PG*, p. 152.
55. *PG*, p. 152.

stoical thinker cannot help but recognize that unity of consciousness and object of consciousness which escaped the servant.

Although stoicism is a new form of consciousness, it does mark a return to an epistemological mode of fulfilling the basic drive of self-consciousness. As illustrated by the preceding development, this drive can be expressed positively as the attempt to have only oneself for an object and thereby to achieve *autonomy* or *self-sufficiency*. It can also be expressed negatively as the attempt to negate the external world and thus become *independent* of it.

For Hegel both the positive and negative expressions are essentially equivalent, and, correspondingly, both the idea of independence and that of autonomy are expressed by Hegel's term—*Selbständigkeit*. To negate the external object is to remove the possibility of having anything but oneself for an object. Put another way, it is to negate the distinction between subject and object.

The basic drive is couched in terms broad enough to be given both epistemological and practical interpretations, and, contrary to Royce, Hegel does not opt for one or the other. This suspension of decision is deliberate and enables Hegel to move from an epistemological stage to a practical one and back to another epistemological one by viewing them as successive attempts to fulfill the same basic drive.

The autonomy and independence sought by the spirit are equated with freedom *(Freiheit)*. Because the stoic is a thinker thinking his own thoughts, self-contained and autonomous, he is free. Because the external world plays no part in this thinking of abstract concepts, he is as a thinker independent of it: "In thought I am free, because I am not in another but remain simply myself."[56]

The stoic has a position in the external world of practical affairs; he may be a master like Marcus Aurelius or a servant like Epictetus, "on the throne or in chains,"[57] but his worldly position is irrelevant to his freedom. Since the external world is not the object or "truth" of the thinking consciousness, "the freedom of self-consciousness is indifferent toward its position in the natural world [*das natürliche Dasein*]"[58]

The servant can become a stoic while outwardly remaining a servant, yet it is misleading to describe this transition as the mere recognition of an independence already possessed by the servant. First, the servant before the transition already recognizes his particular kind of independence when he recognizes himself in the products of his labor. Secondly, the independence of the stoic has a radically different basis from that of the servant; the former is the result of a certain kind of action, while the latter is the result of withdrawing from all action. The independence that the stoic recognizes is not the same one which the servant possessed.

The sort of freedom which a man may possess while in chains is not obvious and contradicts ordinary common sense. Freedom is a notion usually associated with action, and to consider a man free whose range of actions is severely restricted seems strange. Hegel is able to consider the stoic slave free, first, because of the

56. Ibid.
57. *PG*, p. 153.
58. Ibid.

equation of freedom with autonomy and self-sufficiency, and second, because autonomy can be epistemological as well as practical. The stoic's freedom is actually epistemological autonomy.

Royce, committed to the rigid view that Hegel is a pragmatist who in every case reduces thought to its practical significance, is forced to claim: "Stoicism, however, is here viewed in its practical, and not in its theoretical aspects as a doctrine of the world. Practically, stoicism is the attitude of the man who regards all things with which he deals as necessarily subject to his own reason, whether he can control them physically or not."[59] It takes more than a little stretching to consider only practical and not at all theoretical the renunciation of the importance of all overt physical activity as a means to freedom and truth. To be sure, the stoic seeks freedom, but in a peculiarly theoretical manner. The stoic "regards all things with which he deals as necessarily subject to his own reason," but only because he refuses to deal with anything but his own thoughts. If there is any "reduction" in Hegel's discussion, it is not the "reduction" of stoicism from a theoretical to a practical view, but the reduction of freedom from a normally practical concept to a peculiarly theoretical and epistemological one. The only sense in which stoicism is presented as "practical" is the trivial one in which all theoretical views involve *mental activity*. This hardly makes Hegel a pragmatist; he is in this particular section rather somewhat of an antipragmatist.

With sharp sociological and psychological insight Hegel says that, "stoicism, the freedom which goes back

59. Royce, pp. 178–79.

into the pure universality of thought, could appear as a general form of the world spirit only in a time of general fear and servitude but also of general education which had taught men to think."[60] The point seems to be that the frustration of the freedom to act results in the search for a type of freedom immune to such frustration. Where the capacity for abstract thought exists, freedom, outwardly thwarted, is sought in thought. Hegel seems to suggest that the stoic's freedom is what Freud might call a substitute gratification. However, this suggestion, interesting and true as it may be, is not completely consonant with the genesis of stoicism in the *Phenomenology*. Although stoicism arises from servitude rooted in fear, it does not arise because the servant is not allowed to act freely, but because all action proves ultimately futile.

Although in the *Phenomenology* stoicism is associated with a particular kind of worldly milieu and rejected as an inadequate form of consciousness, its concept of freedom as autonomy or self-sufficiency is never rejected by Hegel. In so far as the stoical consciousness *thinks*, it resembles the last stage and goal of the *Phenomenology*, "absolute knowledge," the philosophical consciousness within which Hegel's *Logic* unfolds. The unity of subject and object achieved by a thinker thinking his own thoughts, this epistemological autonomy, is as characteristic of the ultimate philosophical consciousness as it is of the stoical consciousness. And freedom is claimed for the philosophical contemplator of concepts, as it was for the stoic, on the basis of epistemological autonomy.

60. *PG*, p. 153.

Later, in the *Encyclopedia*, in passages reminiscent of the stoic's rejection of action, freedom is still found only in thought: "In logic, thoughts are understood to have no content except that which belongs to and is produced by thinking. Thus, the thoughts are pure thoughts. Thus, the spirit remains with itself and so is free, for freedom is just this: to remain with oneself in its other, to depend on oneself, to determine oneself. In all impulses and appetites (*Trieben*) I begin with an other, with something which is external to me. In this case we speak of dependence. Freedom is only present where there is no other for me, which is not myself."[61] Empirical knowledge—because it requires an external object and is therefore not autonomous—is branded unfree: "While this sensible world [*dies Sinnliche*] is and remains for empiricism something given, empiricism is a doctrine of bondage [*Unfreiheit*], for freedom consists precisely in my having no absolute other opposed to me, but in my depending on a content which I am myself."[62]

Stoicism is not, as Royce suggests,[63] rejected because its freedom is sought in thought rather than in overt action. The self-sufficiency of conceptual thought as the source of freedom is rejected neither at this point nor later. To be sure, Hegel says, "Freedom in thought has only pure thought as its truth which is without the fulfillment of life and therefore only the concept of free-

61. *Enc.*, sec. 24, Z2. See also *Enc.*, sec. 23.
62. *Enc.*, sec. 38, Z.
63. "The dialectical defect of the stoic's position is that the actual world of the stoic's life—the world of activity of desire, of interest—is meanwhile going on in its own accidental way. The self in order to attain independence has resigned all definite plans of control over fortunes" (Royce, p. 179).

dom, not living freedom itself.[64] But the immediately following explication makes clear that what is required to fulfill the concept of freedom is not to abandon thought and return to overt action, but to fill in the general concept of pure thought with a detailed and determinate content of particular thoughts: "However, since individuality should show itself to be alive by acting, or grasp the living world in a system of thought by thinking, there must lie *in thought itself* the contents of the good for action and the contents of the true for thought, so that there is no ingredient other than the concept . . . in all that exists for consciousness."[65]

The autonomy of thought is not to be rejected but saved, and this can only be done if the thinking subject produces not only the general conceptual form of his object but also its specific content. Even if the stoic acts, this action must be directed and determind by *thought*. His failure does not lie in his desertion of action for thought, but in his inability to derive from thought explicit directives for both. It is not action per se which the stoic has neglected but the specificity of both action and thought.

Since the stoical consciousness needs a content and cannot itself provide one, it must accept and depend upon one *given* to it from without. Thus, its autonomy and freedom are lost. The autonomous last stage of the *Phenomenology*, on the contrary, is able to provide its own content, that is, the determinate development of Hegel's *Logic*, and thus maintain its autonomy and freedom.

64. *PG*, p. 153.
65. *PG*, p. 154.

The stoic's wisdom is limited to the knowledge that truth, goodness, and freedom reside in thought. His true but trivial generalizations, that one should know the truth, think thoughts, do the good, and seek virtue and wisdom, make him an uplifting bore. When Polonius asks Hamlet what he is reading, Hamlet answers, "Words"! Hegel's stoic resembles a Hamlet without irony, a man who says and knows only that the book contains words.

SKEPTICISM

Skepticism seeks to correct the inadequacies of stoicism. Since stoicism's fault was not that it sought freedom in thought, there is no return to action. Instead, skepticism is "the realization of that of which stoicism is only the concept—and the actual experience of what *freedom of thought* is."[66] The downfall of the stoic's independence was caused by his need for a specific content and his inability to provide one himself. The skeptic does not, however, solve the problem of content by providing one; instead he explicitly denies the necessity and reality of any specific content. The "remaining determinateness," which the stoic, unable to produce, had to accept as an external given, is for the skeptical consciousness "completely inessential."

Although, in contrast to the ultimate stage of the *Phenomenology*, neither stoicism nor skepticism provides its own specific content, there is a difference between them: what the stoic *ignores*, the skeptic *denies*. Stoicism places no importance on its worldly position;

66. Ibid.

skepticism goes a step further and explicitly denies the reality of this world. Skepticism makes explicit what was implicit in stoicism.

In its negation of the external world skepticism resembles desire and work. But while those attempts to negate through *action* fail, "this polemical course against the manifold independence of things is successful, because it turns against them as an already completed, free self-consciousness, more precisely, because it contains *thought*.[67] Unlike negation through action, denial through thought does not require the presence of the objects it negates. Yet, although the skeptic denies the manifold reality of the external world, he finds himself behaving as if it were real. The skeptical consciousness is schizoid; it contains two conflicting conceptions of itself: "It admits to be an entirely accidental, individual consciousness—a consciousness that is empirical, conforms to what has no reality for it, obeys what has no significance for it, and does and makes real what has no truth for it. But even as it considers itself individual, accidental, animal life, and lost self-consciousness, it also makes itself, on the contrary, general and self-identical, for it is the negativity of all individuality and all distinction."[68]

Hegel also claims that the skeptic's "words and deeds constantly contradict each other" because "it pronounces absolute disappearance, and the pronouncement exists . . .; it pronounces the nullity of seeing, hearing, etc., and it itself sees, hears, etc.; it pronounces the nullity of ethical realities, and acts according to them

67. *PG*, p. 155.
68. *PG*, p. 157.

[*macht sie selbst zu den Mächten seines Handelns*]."[69]

Although Hegel does not develop this line of thought more fully, he certainly supplies stimulus for further reflection. It might be noted that the three arguments offered, despite their obvious similarities, make slightly different points. The first ("It pronounces absolute disappearance, and the pronouncement exists") shows that the actual utterance of a certain skeptical position—that nothing exists—is self-defeating. In this respect it resembles utterances like "I am mute" and "I do not exist."[70] Of course, the skeptic, by not stating his position, could escape this difficulty.

The second argument ("It pronounces the nullity of seeing, hearing, etc., and it itself sees, hears, etc.") is, in one sense, more basic, for it finds fault with those skeptics who, regardless of whether or not they state their positions, continue to perceive the external world, though they deny the reality of both this world and the perception of it. To refrain from perceiving the world is, even for a skeptic, most probably impossible and, at least, much more difficult than simply refraining from stating one's skepticism.

The third argument ("It pronounces the nullity of ethical realities, and acts according to them.") refers to the fact that those skeptical of the validity of moral codes and principles usually follow them anyway. The skeptic can certainly avoid this pitfall by acting amorally; Hegel only argues that, as a matter of fact, they do not.

69. Ibid.
70. It resembles a negative form of A. J. Ayer's version of the *Cogito ergo sum* argument. See Ayer, *The Problem of Knowledge*, pp. 44–52.

However, the general criticism that the skeptic's deeds contradict his words is only obliquely and incompletely exemplified in these three arguments. We are offered the two highly specialized and easily avoidable activities of obeying moral precepts and actually stating the skeptical position, and the very general, if not universal, perception of the external world, which is only dubiously a "deed." The best case for the claim that the skeptic's deeds contradict his words is not made by any of these three arguments, but it is a consequence of the last. The skeptic betrays himself, not only in his philosophical garrulity and moral conventionality, but in the entire range of his normal practical activity, his ordinary reactions to an environment whose existence he denies.

Hegel suggests this more general and forceful objection in describing one of the skeptic's two conceptions of himself as "a consciousness that is empirical" which "conforms to what has no reality for it." We find this more general statement of the manner in which the skeptic's deeds contradict his words in the middle of what seems to be a separate objection.[71] This is not surprising if we give up the idea that the contradiction between the skeptic's words and deeds and his conflicting conceptions of himself are separate points. Their relation is close and simple; the conflicting conceptions arise as the result of the discrepancy between word and deed. One of the skeptic's conceptions of himself is based on his words, that is, his skeptical doctrine; the other on his betrayal of this doctrine in action.

Much the same objection, that the skeptic betrays

71. See Kaufmann, p. 154.

himself in his ordinary and inevitable reaction to the physical environment, is made more clearly in David Hume's *Dialogues Concerning Natural Religion* (1779). There, Cleanthes says to Philo, "Whether your skepticism be as absolute and sincere as you pretend, we shall learn by and by, when the company breaks up; we shall then see whether you go out at the door or the window, and whether you really doubt if your body has gravity or can be injured by its fall, according to popular opinion derived from our fallacious senses and more fallacious experience."[72] Attempting to exit through the door betrays a belief which the skeptic denies having. A point is made of the fantastic difficulty involved in remaining true to this position: "In reality, Philo, continued he, it seems certain that, though a man, in a flush of humour, after intense reflection on the many contradictions and imperfections of human reason, may entirely renounce all belief and opinion, it is impossible for them to persevere in this total skepticism or make it appear in his conduct for a few hours."[73]

Hegel's charge is not merely that the skeptic is inconsistent, but that the willingness to maintain this inconsistency shows a lack of seriousness and sincerity. Also this point is more clearly expressed by Hume: "I shall never assent to so harsh an opinion as that of a celebrated writer [Antoine Arnauld] who says that the skeptics are not a sect of philosophers: they are only a sect of liars. I may, however, affirm (I hope without offence) that they are a sect of jesters or railers."[74] For

72. Hume, *Dialogues Concerning Natural Religion*, p. 7.
73. Ibid., p. 7.
74. Ibid., p. 12.

both Hegel and Hume, the skeptic appears to be like a man who professes asceticism at a banquet. However, Hegel views the skeptic not so much as a liar or jester but as a self-deceiver—what Sartre would consider a case of *mauvaise foi*.

As I have repeatedly tried to show, Royce's thesis that Hegel *everywhere* reduces theory to its practical implications is false. However, the rejection of skepticism follows a roughly Roycean pattern.[75] Although the theory is not reduced to its practical implications, these implications are treated as an integral part of the skeptical position. While Hegel does not make the questionable claim that all theories amount to nothing more than

75. Ironically, Royce fails to point out the pragmatic basis of the very transition capable to some extent of supporting his thesis. Of skepticism, he says, "The result of a thorough-going adoption of this point of view is that life gets the sort of vanity which has been well suggested to our own generation by Fitzgerald's wonderful paraphrase of the Omar Khayyam stanzas" (pp. 179–180). Of the transition from skepticism to the next stage, "The Unhappy Consciousness," he says only, "That the consciousness of the Omar Khayyam stanza is unhappy we shall all remember. And that this unhappiness results from scepticism concerning the worth of every concrete human life, is also obvious" (p. 180). But skepticism falters and becomes an unhappy consciousness just because it cannot completely convince itself that life is in vain and acts instead as if life were worth something. Royce has inverted Hegel here.

Just for the record, Omar Khayyam, far from holding concrete human life to be worthless, finds it to be the only thing of worth. For example, Quatrain XXIII:

Ah, make the most of what we yet may spend,
Before we too into the dust descend,
Dust into Dust, and under Dust, to lie,
Sans Wine, Sans Song, Sans Singer and—sans End!

(Also quatrains II, III, VII) Khayyam is skeptical of any afterworldly reward (XII) and of philosophy because it does nothing to change life (XXII, XXV, XL). The shortness of life is lamented (XIV, XVI, XVII) not because of its vanity, but because of the unique worth of its sensual joys (X, XI).

their practical implications, he sensibly believes that theories do have practical implications, and that to hold a theory seriously and sincerely involves *living* in accordance with it, as well as mouthing it.

Although it seems obvious that being a Buddhist involves more than learning to recite the Four Noble Truths and the Eightfold Path, and being an ascetic more than clever tabletalk, it has not generally been quite so clear that being a skeptic involves any more than the mastery of certain destructive arguments. For this reason, calling attention to the impossibly rigorous behavioral directives involved in skepticism is worth doing.

The same sort of thesis constitutes perhaps the general theme of the philosophy of Søren Kierkegaard, one of Hegel's most prominent and vehement critics. Kierkegaard constantly calls attention to the extremely rigorous and usually ignored implications for life involved in being a Christian. Kierkegaard's point about being a Christian is essentially Hegel's point about being a skeptic: it is much easier said than done.

THE UNHAPPY CONSCIOUSNESS

When the skeptical consciousness becomes aware of the contradiction it contains, it becomes "The Unhappy Consciousness," which through a profusion of rather specific allusions is related to medieval Christianity. In its insistence on the unimportance and unreality of worldly existence Christianity resembles stoicism and skepticism. Each has the negation of the physical world as a goal. While stoicism tries to achieve this goal by ignoring the physical world, and skepticism by denying that it exists, Christianity unhappily accepts the fact of its existence and looks forward to the fulfillment of its goal, independence from the physical world only in an afterlife *(Jenseits)*. Emerging from the self-deception of stoicism and skepticism, the unhappy consciousness faces the fact of its present failure, and hopes instead for future success in an eternal world. But since this other world is defined only negatively as being beyond this one, as a *Jenseits*, "the hope to unite with it must remain a hope, that is, without fulfillment in the present."[76] Adumbrating Nietzsche and Freud, Hegel considers the otherworldliness of Christianity both as a response to failure and an insurance against success.[77]

The unhappy consciousness miserably aware of its physical existence and environment tries to negate them and thus become free from them by renouncing the sensual world and its pleasures. But asceticism fails to achieve its end because

> These [animal functions], instead of being done naturally as something which, in and of itself, is inconsequential and can acquire no importance and essentiality for the spirit, become, since they are viewed as the enemy in his proper form, the object of serious effort and precisely the most important thing. Since, however, this enemy creates himself even in defeat, consciousness is fixated by it and, instead of becoming free of it, constantly dwells upon it and is aware of being constantly defiled. At the same time, this content of its effort is, rather than something essential, the lowest, rather than

76. *PG*, p. 161.
77. See Chap. 4, "Bad Infinity and the Beyond."

something universal, the merest particular. Thus we
see a personality, as unhappy as it is pitiful, limited to
itself and its petty deeds, and brooding over itself.[78]

This is essentially the same criticism of asceticism
offered by Gautama, the Buddha,[79] and also anticipates
some of Nietzsche's remarks on chastity: "Chastity is a
virtue in some, but a vice in many. They abstain but the
bitch, sensuality, leers enviously out of everything they
do. . . . And how nicely the bitch, sensuality, knows how
to beg for a piece of spirit when denied a piece of meat.
. . . And this parable too I offer you: not a few who have
wanted to drive out their devil have themselves entered
into swine.[80]

The unhappy consciousness, because it honestly faces
the problematic existence of the external world rather
than trying to ignore or deny it, is an advance over stoicism and skepticism. But its two attempts to solve the
problem after facing it, asceticism and otherworldliness, are no more successful than either stoicism or skepticism. With the failure of the unhappy consciousness
to negate the physical world and attain the autonomy

78. *PG*, pp. 168–69.
79. The spirit of Hegel's and the Buddha's criticism is neatly captured
in the Zen story, *Muddy Road*: "Tanzan and Ekido were once travelling
together down a muddy road. A heavy rain was still falling. Coming
around a bend, they met a lovely girl in a silk kimono and sash, unable to
cross the intersection. 'Come on girl,' said Tanzan at once. Lifting her up
in his arms, he carried her over the mud. Ekido did not speak again until
that night when they reached a lodging temple. Then he could no longer
restrain himself. 'We monks don't go near females,' he told Tanzan,
'especially not young and lovely ones. It is dangerous. Why did you do
that?' 'I left the girl there,' said Tanzan. 'Are you still carrying her?' " In
Zen Flesh, Zen Bones, ed. Paul Reps, p. 18.
80. *Thus Spoke Zarathustra*, part 1, "On Chastity," in *The Portable
Nietzsche*, trans. Walter Kaufmann, pp. 166–67.

and independence which we have seen to be the elusive goal of all the forms of self-consciousness, the spirit moves on to the third, large section of the *Phenomenology*, "Reason." The spirit returns to forms of consciousness which—like those in Section A, "Consciousness"—appear to be epistemological rather than practical.

However, as I have stressed in this exposition of "Self-consciousness," the task of the spirit is formulated so as to allow for both epistemological and practical attempts at fulfillment. The spirit's goal of practico-epistemological autonomy does not clearly emerge until self-consciousness is attained, for its introduction depends on the notion of self-consciousness. Yet this goal is neither relinquished with the transition from "Self-consciousness" to "Reason" nor later in the *Phenomenology*. This is not surprising, for, just as the stages of the *Phenomenology* occurring after the section titled "Consciousness" are still forms of consciousness, the stages occurring after the section titled "Self-consciousness" are still forms of self-consciousness.[81] Given this goal, it is again not surprising that the remainder of the *Phenomenology* exhibits that alternation of modes of knowing and of acting so typical of the section titled "Self-consciousness."

Certainly, it is interesting and worthwhile to attempt to construct a general theory of human behavior which encompasses both endeavors, to know and to act. Merely because both Hegel and the pragmatists make such an attempt, we should not conclude with Royce that Hegel is a pragmatist. There are obvious ways of relating thought and action other than reducing

81. See Appendix.

the former to the latter: what we think and know influences how we act, and experience gathered in action helps determine what we think and know. Tracing relationships of this sort in no way bizarre or objectionable and can be fruitful. But Hegel, as we have seen, does more than this; he considers all the different forms of knowing and acting, all the exertions of the human spirit, as expressions of the same basic drive, the drive toward autonomy and self-sufficiency. In this lies the real "reduction" of the *Phenomenology* and the root of the book's linear development.

We have seen how the concept of *autonomy* easily and naturally runs into that of *freedom*, and how freedom, usually a practical concept, is released from its binding associations with action and also equated with epistemological autonomy. Freedom acquires that practico-epistemological duality characteristic of the basic goal of the spirit and, in fact, becomes *synonomous* with this goal. The spirit seeks freedom (in its expanded sense).

Yet the efforts of the spirit culminate in philosophy, and the goal of philosophy and thus of the spirit in general was not said to be freedom but *truth*. However, this is only a superficial inconsistency. Just as the concept *freedom* was expanded by 'epistemologizing' it, the concept of truth is expanded by 'pragmatizing' it. As I have pointed out,[82] this expansions involves two major steps: (1) in addition to its normal use as the contrary of falsity, truth is also used as synonym for the *object* of consciousness and opposed not to falsity but to the conscious subject. What the subject knows or is

82. See Chap. 1, "Self-consciousness."

conscious of is for Hegel its "truth." (2) When the form of consciousness is active rather than contemplative, its object (*Gegenstand*) is really an objective or goal. Once the object of a form of consciousness has already been identified as its "truth," it is but a small additional step also to identify the objective of an activity as its "truth."

The spirit can now seek truth both through contemplation and through action. The concept *truth* acquires that same practico-epistemological duality characteristic of *autonomy, self-sufficiency,* and *freedom,* which enables it to join them as an alternative expression for the general goal of human endeavor.

There remains one difficulty. Although truth comes to share this practico-epistemological character with autonomy, self-sufficiency, and freedom, it does not seem to have any other conceptual similarity to them, while they seem to be roughly synonomous with each other in Hegel's philosophy. If truth is not somehow identified conceptually with these other expressions of the basic goal, then despite his efforts to give each of them the prerequisite duality Hegel is still guilty of offering two different things as the one basic goal of the human spirit.

However, Hegel does try to identify truth with freedom and autonomy. We have seen how he argues that freedom is found only in conceptual thought.[83] He also argues that truth is to be found only in conceptual thought because only there is consciousness autonomous and free. It remains to be seen how freedom, even in the sense of epistemological autonomy, is argued

83. See Chap. 1, "Stoicism."

to be necessary for knowing the truth. In other words, why must genuine knowledge be self-knowledge? To answer that only self-knowledge is autonomous and thus free is to beg the question. What must be shown is why only knowledge which is autonomous and free is truly knowledge.

Hegel's arguments to this end are motivated and to some extent justified by his attempt to resolve the problem of knowing things as they are in themselves, Kant's onerous legacy to his philosophic successors. In the next chapter I shall discuss Hegel's struggle with this problem.

2 ~ THE PROBLEM OF THE THING-IN-ITSELF

Hegel stresses the fact that philosophy's goal is the goal of all human endeavor and characterizes this goal very generally as the truth. Yet he ranks the various forms of human activity; and philosophy, as evidenced by its terminal position both in the *Phenomenology* and the *Encyclopedia,* emerges as the highest form of this common endeavor—the fullest realization of truth. With this exalted position come more rigorous requirements. The philosopher, like everyone else, seeks truth, but the philosopher cannot be satisfied with anything less than the highest form of truth.

By characterizing the object of each form of consciousness as its truth, Hegel subtly reinforces and draws upon his thesis that each form of consciousness, despite its inadequacies, has some degree of success and contains some degree of truth. But although each has truth as its object, each has it in a different form. Philosophy "is different from other ways of becoming conscious of this one and the same content only in form,"[1] and philosophy's task is more precisely to seek "the true form in which the truth exists."[2] The sublime truth of philosophy is identified throughout Hegel's works as "the absolute-truth"[3] or more often simply as *the absolute (das Absolute)* : "The history of philosophy is the history of the discovery of thoughts about the absolute,

1. *Enc.,* sec. 6.
2. *PG,* p. 12.
3. *Logic,* 1:41.

47

which is its object."[4] For philosophy, "the principle in which alone the interest of the matter seems to lie is the interest as to what is the truth, the absolute ground of everything."[5]

Since philosophy's goal is nothing less than "the highest truth,"[6] truth without any of the limitations characteristic of the other forms of knowledge, it is not surprising that philosophy requires a special method of its own. Philosophy is the final form of a relentless drive toward truth which can accept no limitation to its scope or to its certainty. Therefore, Hegel, along with his thesis about the community of all human endeavor, can still emphasize the inadequacy of philosophic methods borrowed from other disciplines, such as mathematics and the empirical sciences. He can claim to offer "a new reworking of philosophy, presented according to a method which is still going to be recognized, I hope, as the only true one, the only one identical with its content."[7]

Other methods are rejected for philosophy because they are incapable of attaining absolute truth. Implicit in this rejection and the search for a new and adequate method is the belief that absolute truth, complete, necessary, free of all limitation, is an attainable or at least tenable goal. Since Immanuel Kant had denied the possibility of such absolute, unlimited knowledge in his *Critique of Pure Reason* (1781), Hegel's entire program and conception of philosophy depended upon re-

4. *Enc.*, Preface, p. 10.
5. *Logic*, 1:51.
6. *Logic*, 1:31.
7. *Enc.*, Preface, 1st ed., p. 20.

futing Kant's limitation of reason. More specifically, Kant had claimed that we can know things only as they appear to us, but never as they really are in themselves. Hegel could not accept this restriction of knowledge and devoted a great deal of his time and energy to removing it. This problem assumed tremendous importance for Hegel.

Ascertaining the relative importance for Hegel of various philosophers is a reasonable and fruitful undertaking, but only if the complexity of this question is realized and no simplistic linear ranking sought. It is not difficult to select with some accuracy a group of the most important influences; certainly Plato, Aristotle, Spinoza, and Kant would be included. But it would be difficult to rank them, for, not surprisingly, each influenced him in a different way and on different issues. Hegel probably derived more of his terminology from Aristotle than from anyone else, yet his idea of the dialectic was inspired more by Plato and Kant, and his central concepts of freedom and infinity stem from Spinoza.

Individual commentators have emphasized different influences; Josiah Royce[8] and Richard Kroner[9] trace the relationship to Kant. G. R. G. Mure devotes a third of his *Introduction to Hegel* to discussing the relevant parts of Aristotle's philosophy. Henry Alonzo Myers devotes his *Hegel or Spinoza* to a comparison and contrast of the two. These varied approaches complement rather than conflict with one another.

Walter Kaufmann, in a more varied and balanced

8. *Lectures on Modern Idealism*
9. *Von Kant bis Hegel.*

approach, traces many of the influences on Hegel and then soundly suggests that the apportionment of space in Hegel's *History of Philosophy* is indicative of the relative importance for Hegel of the various philosophers.[10] By this criterion Kant runs a poor third to Plato and Aristotle, each of whom is given over twice as much space as Kant.

Although this apportionment is indeed "surprising but revealing," it is also misleading if taken as the only index of Kant's importance for Hegel. (Kaufmann does not claim that it is.) This particular bit of evidence has the attraction of being comprehensive and quantitative, but a consideration of the *Phenomenology*, *Science of Logic*, and *Encyclopedia* furnishes evidence which, though not as neat, is still relevant and modifies the picture derived solely from the *History of Philosophy*.

In these works a philosopher's importance cannot be measured solely by the amount of explicit reference made to him. Since the *Phenomenology* relies on allusion rather than explicit reference, counting the rare references which do occur is extremely unreliable. In both the *Science of Logic* and the *Encyclopedia*, where more abundant references form a more reliable index, Kant's is the name mentioned most often.[11] Still, statistics of this sort furnish only a purview of Kant's importance for Hegel.

Hegel's estimation of Kant's stature and importance appears clearly in a footnote to the *Science of Logic*: "I am calling attention to the fact that I often take the

10. Kaufmann, sec. 66, pp. 278–81.
11. Based on the *Personenregister* at the back of the *Kritische Ausgabe*, edited by J. Hoffmeister.

Kantian philosophy into consideration in this work (which could appear superfluous to many), because no matter how its smaller details and the particular parts of its development may be regarded in this work and elsewhere, it constitutes the basis and point of departure of the modern German philosophy."[12]

In any case, it is not important to argue whether Kant was the single greatest influence on Hegel. It is more interesting to see exactly how, rather than how much, Kant influenced Hegel. Kant's denial of the possibility of knowing things-in-themselves (*Dinge-an-sich*) poses one of the major problems for both the *Phenomenology* and the later system. This problem haunts Hegel's philosophy, which is, to a large extent, an attempt to solve it.

Following the famous "Preface" to the *Phenomenology* there is a shorter "Introduction" in which the problem of knowing things as they are in themselves is the major theme. The "Introduction" (unlike the "Preface" which was added later) was written immediately prior to the main body of the work and reveals the concerns with which Hegel approached that undertaking:

> It is natural to suppose that, before philosophy enters upon its subject proper, namely the actual knowledge of what truly is, it is necessary first to understand knowledge, which is considered the tool with which one masters the absolute, or the medium through which one catches sight of it. . . . This concern necessarily transforms itself into the conviction that the whole undertaking to gain for consciousness a knowledge of that which

12. *Logic*, 1:44.

is in-itself [*was an sich ist*] is absurd in its conception,
and that between knowledge and the absolute a barrier
falls which completely separates them. For if knowledge
is the tool with which to master the absolute, it is immediately apparent that the application of a tool to
something does not leave it as it is for itself but undertakes to form and change it. Or if knowledge is not the
tool of our activity but to some extent a passive medium
through which the light of truth reaches us, we do
not receive it as it is in itself, but as it is through and in
this medium. In both cases we use a means which immediately brings about the opposite of its end; or rather
the absurdity is that we use a means at all. It seems, of
course, that this difficulty can be remedied by knowing
how the tool works, for it would then be possible to subtract from the notion of the absolute which we receive
by means of the tool the part which belongs to the tool,
and thus receive the pure truth. But this improvement
would, in fact, only bring us back to where we were before. If we take away from a formed thing what the tool
has done to it, then the thing—here, the absolute—is
again exactly what it was before this now obviously
superfluous effort. . . . Or if the examination of knowledge, which we now represent to ourselves as a medium,
taught us the law of its refraction, it would be of no
use to subtract the refraction from the result, for knowledge is not the refraction of the ray, but the ray itself
through which the truth contacts us. With this removed, only the bare direction or the empty place
would be indicated to us.[13]

Although Kant is not explicitly mentioned, and the
metaphors of the tool and the medium replace the Kant-

13. *PG*, pp. 63–64.

ian terminology, Hegel is referring to Kant's denial of the possibility to know things as they are in themselves. The absence of explicit reference is not unusual in the *Phenomenology*, and there is an obvious kinship between this passage and passages in the *Science of Logic* and the *Encyclopedia* which clearly refer to Kant or the "Critical Philosophy." For example: "A major viewpoint of the *Critical Philosophy* is that, before one attempts to know God, the essence of things, etc., one must first investigate the capacity of knowledge itself, to see whether it is able to accomplish such tasks. One must first become acquainted with the *instrument*, before one undertakes the work which is to be accomplished by means of it. Otherwise, if the instrument were inadequate, all efforts would be wasted and in vain."[14]

There also is an obvious reason for the metaphorical presentation. At this point Hegel does not try to refute Kant's denial directly. Instead, he suggests that this denial draws support from *unexamined* and *misleading metaphors*: "In fact, this fear of error assumes something, indeed quite a lot, as true, and supports its scruples and conclusions on what should itself be examined for its truth beforehand. It unquestioningly represents [*setzt Vorstellungen voraus*] knowledge as a tool and a medium and presupposes a distinction between ourselves and this knowledge."[15]

Hegel admits that the metaphors of the tool or the medium, once accepted, lead inexorably to the conclusion that we cannot know things as they are in them-

14. *Enc.*, sec. 10.
15. *PG*, pp. 64–65.

selves. But he denies that we must, or even should, accept these models for knowledge. He is adamant both about the unacceptability of the consequences of these metaphors and the complete lack of any justification for their use.

Knowledge limited to phenomena, the knowledge offered by Kant, is spurned. For Hegel, this kind of knowledge is not only ultimately unsatisfying, but does not even deserve to be called knowledge. In the *Phenomenology* he says,

> This fear of error principally presupposes that the absolute stands on one side, and that knowledge, on the other side, by itself and separated from the absolute, is still something real, or that knowledge, which being outside of the absolute is also outside of the truth, is still true knowledge. This assumption reveals what calls itself the fear of error to be rather the fear of the truth.
>
> This conclusion follows from the fact that the absolute alone is true, or the true alone is absolute. It can be denied by making a distinction allowing knowledge which does not, as science requires, know the absolute to be true knowledge also. [Or one might consider that] knowledge in general, though unable to grasp the absolute, is still capable of another truth.[16]

Here, Hegel is content to point out that salvaging a limited truth, like the use of the tool and medium metaphors, depends upon ideas and distinctions which are never examined. The need for conceptual analysis is stressed: "But we see immediately that such aimless talk stems from a murky distinction between an abso-

16. *PG*, p. 65.

lute truth and some other kind of truth, and 'absolute,'
'knowledge,' etc., are words which presuppose meanings which first have to be obtained."[17] If these words
and distinctions are not first analyzed and their use
justified, one can, he argues, just as well blindly ignore
them as blindly accept them.

Hegel asserts that one has even *more* right to ignore
them than to accept them, for they produce "only an
empty appearance of knowledge, which disappears immediately when science arrives." This is a heuristic
point: *in the absence of any justification either for accepting or rejecting these metaphors,* one should ignore
them and try to develop the science which knows things
as they are in themselves. If one succeeds, the metaphors and the limitation of knowledge which follows
from them will be rejected or, as Hegel puts it, "will
immediately disappear." If on the contrary, one uncritically accepts the impossibility of absolute knowledge, no such effort will be made.

In the *Science of Logic,* knowledge limited to phenomena is rejected not only because it rests on unan-
alyzed concepts and strangles philosophic progress, but
also because it is a notion which crumbles upon examination. It poses as a kind of knowledge but really is not.

Since . . . this knowledge knows itself to be only knowledge of appearances, it admits to be unsatisfactory. Yet,
it is assumed at the same time that things, though not
rightly known in themselves, are still rightly known
within the sphere of appearance, as though only the
kinds of objects were different, and one kind, namely
things in themselves, did not fall within knowledge, but

17. Ibid.

the other kind, namely appearances, did. How would
it be to attribute accurate perception to a man, with
the proviso that he was not able to perceive truth but
only untruth? As absurd as that would be, a true knowledge which did not know its object as it is in itself would
be equally absurd.[18]

Things as they are in themselves and things as they
appear to us are not merely two kinds of objects; the
former are things as they truly are, the latter are things
but not as they truly are. Thus, to know things only as
they appear to us and not as they are in themselves is
to know things but not as they truly are. Hegel doubts
whether this can be considered knowledge at all. Again
the heuristic motive is operative: accepting the false
consolation of this pseudoknowledge dulls our drive for
·genuine knowledge.

It might seem that Hegel, without any justification,
denies that things appear to us as they truly are. But
Hegel has not, in the preceding argument, even committed himself to this view. He asserts only that, *if*
the distinction between things in themselves and things
as they appear is accepted, then appearances are contrasted with the things as they are in themselves, that
is, with things as they truly are. The falsity of appearances is only argued to be a consequence of the very
distinction Hegel tries to refute.[19]

Given the distinction between things as they are in
themselves and things as they appear to us, and their

18. *Logic*, 1:27.
19. Since empiricism does not contrast appearances with things as they
really are, Hegel never charges it with not *seeking* genuine knowledge, even
though it uses the appearance of things as its basis.

respective truth and falsity, Hegel's refusal to consider knowledge of appearances to be truly knowledge is not idiosyncratic. Hegel argues that, if what is 'known' is not true, it is not really known. Essentially the same point is made by A. J. Ayer when he claims that a necessary condition for knowledge is that "what one is said to know be true."[20] And as Ayer is quick to add, this is a common sense view: "For while what is true can be believed, or disbelieved, or doubted, or imagined, or much else besides being known, it is, as we have already noted, a fact of ordinary usage that what is known, in this sense, cannot but be true."[21]

Unlike Ayer, Hegel does not support this particular point by explicitly appealing to common opinion or ordinary linguistic usage. Yet, in discussing the general problem of knowing things as they are in themselves he does consider common opinion and usage.

After characterizing the current and unacceptable view as one in which "thought, in its relation to the object, does not come out of itself toward the object, which remains, as a thing in itself, simply something beyond thought [*ein Jenseits des Denkens*]"; Hegel candidly admits that "these views of the relation between subject and object express the determinations which constitute the nature of our ordinary conscious-

20. *The Problem of Knowledge* (Edinburgh, Penguin Books, 1956) p. 35.
21. Ibid, p. 12. The sense of knowing that Ayer refers to is knowing that something is the case, which he is careful to distinguish from knowledge in the sense of acquaintance, and Hegel, in talking about knowing things, seems rather to be discussing the latter. But the difference between them is diminished if it is remembered that Hegel does not make such a distinction, and that much of our knowledge by acquaintance can be easily translated into knowledge that something is the case.

ness."[22] The subject-object distinction which leads to the Kantian limitation of knowledge is here said to have a basis in ordinary thought, not to justify it, but merely to explain its prevalence. Hegel admits that this distinction is widely accepted, but he still maintains that it is an unexamined "prejudice," unfit for philosophy. The implications are clear: popularity is not a sufficient criterion for philosophical truth; popular notions must be subjected to analysis and criticism.

Although Hegel does not consider ordinary opinion and usage the ultimate arbiter of philosophic problems, he occasionally draws supplementary support from this quarter. This procedure may seem arbitrary, inconsistent, and even dishonest. What right does Hegel have to use only that part of ordinary opinion and usage which confirms his theories and to reject the rest? However, as long as ordinary opinion and usage are used only as *supplementary* sources of philosophical enlightenment, Hegel's occasional appeal to them is quite consistent with his rejection of their ultimate authority. In fact, this procedure itself follows the dictates of good common sense. Ordinary opinion and usage, like the theories and idiom of any great, extraordinary philosopher, are to be used selectively and in conjunction with other considerations. Rejecting parts of ordinary opinion and usage is more like occasionally rejecting the opinion of a generally reliable adviser than it is like rejecting unpleasant experimental data.

The sharp separation of subject and object, knower and known, thought and its object, may have roots in ordinary opinion and usage, but the Kantian limitation

22. *Logic*, 1:25.

of knowledge which results from this separation does not. In the *Logic*, an attack of an admittedly popular belief is unabashedly followed by: "On the other hand, however, one can appeal to the characteristic *ideas of ordinary logic*; it is assumed that definitions, for example, do not contain determinations which fall only in the knowing subject, but determinations of the object, which constitute its most essential and inmost nature."[23] In the *Encyclopedia*, this same confidence in the ability of thought to know things in themselves is claimed to be even more extensive: "All incipient philosophy, all of the sciences, even the daily deeds and drives of consciousness live in this belief."[24]

Consequently Kant's theory runs counter to common sense: "It has been said that things in themselves are quite different from what we make out of them. In particular, the Critical Philosophy has gained acceptance for this divorce between thought and thing despite the conviction of the entire previous world that their agreement was a matter of course."[25]

This common belief is said to be "of the greatest importance" and the task of philosophy to be a return to the ordinary and—in this instance—sound view: "The business of philosophy consists only in explicitly bringing to consciousness what, in retrospect, has prevailed in human thought for ages. Philosophy therefore advances nothing new; what we have here brought out through reflection is already the immediate prejudice of

23. *Logic*, 1:32.
24. *Enc.*, sec. 26. The reference to the beliefs implicit in our everyday activity echoes the criticism made of skepticism in the *Phenomenology*. See above, Chap. 1, "Skepticism."
25. *Enc.*, sec. 22, Z.

everyone."[26] Despite the unrestricted formulation of the passage, Hegel's open condemnation of many common sense views makes it clear that he is here presenting not a description of philosophic method in general, but only of proper procedure in one instance.

In an even more contemporary tone, ordinary *usage*, not just ordinary *opinion*, is invoked: "In general, it lies at the very basis of the use of such forms as the concept, the judgment, the inference, the definition, the division, etc., that they are forms not only of self-conscious thought, but also of the objective world."[27] Since Hegel later criticizes some of these same forms,[28] the appeal to ordinary usage, like the appeal to ordinary belief, must be viewed merely as an added inducement to be dissatisfied with Kant's position and to examine it critically.

The fact that Kant's limitation of knowledge, which contradicts common sense, is based on metaphors and distinctions that are rooted in common sense, shows that common sense, far from being faultless, may have implications that it cannot itself accept. It supports the demand that philosophy analyze ordinary belief in order to bring these implications and inconsistencies to light.

That Hegel would resort to ordinary opinion and usage despite his reservations about this approach is another indication of the great importance he placed upon the problem of knowing things as they really are in themselves. As we have seen, Kant's limitation of knowledge seems completely to undermine the quest for ab-

26. *Enc.*, sec. 22, Z.
27. *Logic*, 1:32.
28. See, e.g., *Enc.*, sec. 31.

solute truth, which, for Hegel, was the ultimate goal
of both philosophy and the human spirit.

Kant's view had to be criticized in order to make Hegel's philosophic program tenable. Therefore, it is not
surprising to find that Hegel devotes much space and
effort to this problem in the introductory sections of the
Phenomenology, Science of Logic and *Encyclopedia.*
To gain sympathy for his program Hegel first had to
silence the predictable Kantian objections to any talk of
knowing things as they really are. Or, as Hegel says in
the "Introduction" to the *Logic,* because this limitation
of knowledge "obstructs the entrance to philosophy," it
must be "sloughed off before philosophy."[29]

The problem posed by Kant's limitation of knowledge loomed large for Hegel not only because of the
unpalatable consequences of Kant's view but also because of its prevalence in the philosophical world. The
already mentioned appraisal of Kant as "the basis and
point of departure of the modern German philosophy"
is immediately justified by reference to the currency
of Kant's limitation of reason: "The philosophizing
which is widest spread among us does not get beyond
the Kantian results, that reason cannot possibly know
a true content, and with regard to absolute truth must
be referred to faith."[30]

Hegel prefaces the *Encyclopedia* by a compressed
historical *Vorbegriff* in which he limns the development
of philosophy preceding him in terms of those problems
and positions most relevant to his own thought. Because the *Vorbegriff* functions as an introduction to

29. *Logic,* 1:25.
30. *Logic,* 1:44.

Hegel's System and is much shorter than Hegel's other account of this same development in his lectures on the *History of Philosophy*, it is more selective than the lectures and better indicates what aspects of Hegel's predecessors most influenced and disturbed him. The *Vorbegriff* has the further advantage of being actually written by Hegel; the *History of Philosophy* was compiled from students' lecture notes.

The entire presentation is permeated by the concern about whether thought is capable of knowing things as they really are. Hegel indicates the importance of this concern by titling each of the *Vorbegriff's* three sections an "attitude of thought to objectivity" (*Stellung des Gedankens zur Objectivität*). This historical introduction is divided into "Metaphysics," "Empiricism," "Critical Philosophy," and "Immediate Knowledge," which are then condensed into three sections by somewhat arbitrarily grouping "Empiricism" and "Critical Philosophy" together.

The section on metaphysics certainly is meant to refer specifically to modern rationalism (Descartes, Leibniz, Spinoza, etc.), but not only to modern rationalism. The defining characteristic of "Metaphysics" is the pre-Kantian confidence in the power of thought to know reality: "The first attitude . . . contains the belief that through reflection truth is known, that what the object truly is is brought before consciousness."[31] As we have seen, this characteristic is generally attributed to "all incipient philosophy" as well as all of science and ordinary activity. But this widespread view has its "most explicit development, and the one nearest to us, in former

31. *Enc.*, sec. 26.

metaphysics, as it was among us before Kant."[32] How far back in time this metaphysics extends is unimportant; it is essentially pre-Kantian.

Hegel's perspective is different from our present one. We tend to view the rationalist confidence in reason as having been undermined by the British empiricists led by Hume and then somewhat restored by Kant. Hegel, on the contrary, sees Kant as further developing the criticism of reason which the empiricists had only begun. For Hegel, Kant's limited restoration of reason was so limited as to be no restoration at all. This may partially explain why Empiricism and Critical Philosophy are grouped together.

Empiricism, "which instead of seeking truth in thought [*Gedanken*], goes to fetch it from experience,"[33] still seeks a truth which, for it, is the only truth there is. Unencumbered by the distinction between knowledge of appearances and knowledge of things in themselves, it considers the experiential knowledge it seeks to be the only and therefore absolute truth. Hegel saw empiricism, not so much as a criticism of all metaphysics, but merely as a different kind of metaphysics, one which held that reality was revealed in experience, and not in abstract thought. The empiricists are criticized for not realizing that their view "itself contains metaphysics"; Hegel calls this "the basic deception of scientific empiricism."

The crushing blow to metaphysics was administered not by empiricism but by Kant: "In common with empiricism the Critical Philosophy takes experience to be

32. *Enc.*, sec. 27.
33. *Enc.*, sec. 37.

the only basis for knowledge, which, however, it does not allow to count as truth, but only as knowledge of appearances."[34] Empiricism only set up the destruction of metaphysics and absolute knowledge which was carried out by Kant.

In this presentation Kant certainly overshadows his predecessors; metaphysics is characterized as essentially pre-Kantian, empiricism as proto-Kantian. And Kant is allotted more than twice as much space as the other two combined.[35]

Hegel also thought that Kant's limitation of knowledge had played a crucial role in the development of a post-Kantian, Romantic rejection of reason—exemplified by Jacobi. Although, like Hegel, Jacobi was unsatisfied by the limited knowledge offered by Kant, unlike Hegel, he completely swallowed Kant's limitation of reason. Thus he was forced to claim that reality could be known in a nonconceptual way. Since the criticism of absolute knowledge that Jacobi accepted represented thought as a means to truth that only made truth inaccessible, he tried to reach truth without thought or any other self-defeating means (*Mittel*). He sought to know truth directly. Hence Hegel calls this section "Immediate Knowledge" (*Das Unmittelbare Wissen*).

34. *Enc.*, sec. 40.

35. Reading Kaufmann's section 66 (pp. 278–81) will remove any inclination to deplore Hegel's provincialism in this matter. Kaufmann argues that Berkeley and Hume would have been given even less consideration in England at that time, and that the later English interest in Berkeley and Hume was initiated by English admirers of Kant and Hegel.

It is also interesting that this apportionment reverses the emphasis in the *History of Philosophy*, where Greek philosophy is given twice as much space as modern philosophy. Perhaps the existence of both treatments alleviates the radical appearance of each.

The consequent reliance on direct intuition, inspiration, ineffable insight, edification, and feeling is often attacked vehemently by Hegel, especially in the "Preface" to the *Phenomenology*. However, what interests us here is not the details of the attack, but the fact that Hegel viewed one major theme and malaise of post-Kantian philosophy to be the result of *accepting* Kant's limitation of conceptual knowledge to phenomena.[36]

Although Kant's doctrine is held to be largely responsible for the subsequent flight from reason to faith and mysticism, Hegel respects Kant more than his romantic successors: "But one immediately begins in this philosophizing with what, for Kant, was a result, and thereby cuts away beforehand the preceding exposition out of which that result came, and which is philosophical knowledge."[37]

Kant's position, wrong and pernicious as it might be, is at least presented as the result of a demonstration, which itself displays philosophical merit and serious effort. Hegel finds the wide, uncritical acceptance of Kant's doctrine suspicious. For those who find conceptual thought too taxing, the doctrine of its metaphysical futility offers a tempting excuse to give it up. Intellectual sloth explains the mysterious popularity of an apparently unpalatable view: "The Kantian philosophy thus serves as a pillow for intellectual indolence which soothes itself with the idea that everything has

36. Hegel is concerned only with what he considered one major trend in post-Kantian philosophy, not with all of it. Post-Kantian idealism (Fichte and perhaps Schelling) was exempted from this particular criticism. See *Logic*, 1:28, quoted early in Chapter 3.
37. *Logic*, 1:44.

been already proved and done away with."[38] In the *Phenomenology* Hegel views the arguments for "the impotence of science" based upon unexamined metaphors to amount to "subterfuges" (*Ausreden*), which are motivated by the desire "to free oneself from the effort of science and, at the same time, to give oneself the appearance of a serious and passionate striving."[39] Surely Kant's successors, and not Kant himself, are being criticized here.

But laziness and pretense aside, it is the rejection of thought's ability to know ultimate reality, common to both Kant and his successors, which seemed to Hegel the major contemporary philosophical issue. He says of the opposition of thought and its object: "Around this opposition revolves the interest of modern philosophy."[40] More elaborately: "Around its nature and validity revolve the interest of the philosophical standpoint of our present time and the question about truth and the knowledge of truth."[41] And this obsession seems justified by the gravity of the issue: "It is the sickness of our time to despair of ever knowing more than something subjective."[42]

THE THING-IN-ITSELF AND KANT'S PHILOSOPHY

Sometimes Hegel's generally sympathetic approach to the history of philosophy and his great respect for Kant lead him to consider this problematic and pernicious doctrine not to be an essential part of Kant's phi-

38. Ibid.
39. *PG*, p. 65.
40. *Enc.*, sec. 22, Z.
41. *Enc.*, sec. 25.
42. *Enc.*, sec. 22, Z

losophy. In an early essay on *The Difference between
the Fichtean and Schellingian Systems of Philosophy*
(1801) he relies on Fichte's distinction between the
spirit and the letter of Kant's philosophy to divide the
wheat from the chaff: "The Kantian philosophy had
required that its spirit be separated from its letter, and
that the purely speculative principle be lifted out of the
rest which belonged to argumentative [*raisonnieren-
den*] reflection *or could be used for it.*"[43] We have seen
with what contempt Hegel considered the post-Kantian
use of the *Ding-an-sich* doctrine. The desire not to
blame Kant for the sins of his successors was probably
one motive for adopting Fichte's distinction.

Another was the belief that Fichte had indeed successfully winnowed Kant's philosophy. Hegel continues: "In the principle of the deduction of the categories this philosophy is genuine idealism, and it is this
principle that Fichte lifted out in purer, more rigorous
form and called the spirit of the Kantian philosophy."[44]

First and foremost among the chaff is the *Ding-an-
sich* doctrine: "That things-in-themselves (which are
nothing but the empty form of opposition [of subject
and object] objectively expressed) are hypostasized and
set up as absolute objectivity, like the things of the dog-
matic philosophers, . . . and only with more pretension
called 'Critical Philosophy'—these conditions lie at
most in the form of the Kantian deduction of the categories, not in its principle or spirit."[45]

While it is sound procedure to admire a great phi-

43. G (*See* Abbreviations), 1:33.
44. G, 1:33–34.
45. G, 1:34.

losopher selectively, distinguishing the valuable elements in his thought from the worthless ones, the true
theses from the false, and the valid arguments from the
fallacious, one should not confuse the procedure with
the question of what the philosopher "really meant" or
felt was most important. Since the confusion of evaluation and interpretation often results in apologetics, the
more a philosopher is revered, the more likely is this
confusion. The distinction between the spirit and the
letter of Kant's philosophy is a misguided attempt to
emphasize his greatness by subtly disassociating him
from what seem to be his less fortunate doctrines. What
is found to be inferior is said to be not essential, not
really meant, or only the letter and not the spirit of the
philosophy. These idioms cloak the entry of indirect
and unjustified apologetics.

Typically, what the apologist finds to be the superior
essence or spirit of the revered philosophy is his own
view; old icons are refurbished only to serve as mirrors:
"In that deduction of the forms of the understanding
the principle of speculation, the identity of subject and
object, is expressed most distinctly."[46] An already devious apologetics can serve as an even more devious
summoning of support from respected sources.

I am not suggesting that these general tendencies are
peculiar to Fichte and Hegel or that they need be conscious strategies. They are to be viewed rather as omni-
present pressures to which any historian of philosophy
might succumb without ever becoming aware of their
presence. These pressures are understandably strongest
where the commentator feels his own work to be the

46. Ibid.

extension or fulfillment of the other man's philosophy, and Fichte held his task to be the completion of what Kant had started.

Hegel, who early in his career adopts from Fichte this manner of discussing Kant, does not continue to use it. In the Preface to the first edition of the *Science of Logic* (1812) Hegel still blames the "decline of metaphysics" and the "strange spectacle of a cultured people without metaphysics" on "the exoteric teaching of the Kantian philosophy—that understanding dare not transcend experience."[47] However, no contrast between an exoteric and an esoteric teaching is developed, and Hegel seems here to be referring primarily to the popularity and influence of this particular doctrine. Furthermore, in the Introduction to the same work the insistence on the subjectivity of knowledge is called Kant's "chief thought" (*Hauptgedanken*). And in the *Encyclopedia* Kant's position is epitomized in terms of this doctrine. Despite a continuing respect for Kant, Hegel clearly finds him responsible for a good part of the "sickness of our time."

THE "PHENOMENOLOGY" AND THE PROBLEM OF THE THING-IN-ITSELF

Removing the limitation of knowledge posed by the *Ding-an-sich* doctrine was for Hegel a necessary propaedeutic to philosophy, and thus his introductions are permeated with this problem. There is one introduction of which this is true that has not yet been considered— the entire *Phenomenology*.

Although the *Phenomenology* was originally con-

47. *Logic*, 1:3.

ceived as the first part of a *System of Science*, to be followed by a second part containing a logic, philosophy of nature, and philosophy of the spirit, Hegel's conception soon changed. The logic, intended to be the first third of the second part, grew so large that it had to be published in three separate volumes.[48] But there was a stronger reason why Hegel never referred to any or all of his later work as the second part of the System. After all, he did eventually publish an *Encyclopedia* of *the Philosophical Sciences*[49] which in one condensed volume contains everything originally planned for the second part of the System. Yet the *Encyclopedia* is presented not as the second part of the System, but as the entire System.

This happened because Hegel came to consider the *Phenomenology* an *introduction* to his system of philosophical science rather than its first part. This change of view is not radical and involves only a slight shift of emphasis and terminology. Even as the first part of the System the *Phenomenology*'s function was to prepare the way for the second part.

The prevalent doubts about the possibility of knowledge of things-in-themselves is mentioned by Hegel at the very beginning of the Introduction to the *Phenomenology* and traced to several unexamined metaphors and an equally unexamined distinction between the knowing subject and its object. Although attention is called to the uncritical way in which the metaphors and the corresponding distinction had been accepted, no refutation is offered in the Introduction itself. However,

48. 1812, 1813, 1816. In the critical edition edited by Lasson there are about 900 pages of text.
49. First Edition, 1817.

given these prevalent doubts, the possibility of a science that can know things as they really are had to be demonstrated. The entire course of the *Phenomenology* is offered as such a demonstration.

Starting with the ordinary view that the conscious subject is separate and distinct from its object, Hegel tries to show how the spirit is forced to reject one form of consciousness after another until this separation is completely overcome in the last stage, "Absolute Knowledge." According to Hegel, the denial of knowledge of things-in-themselves rests on the separation of the knowing subject from its object. Therefore, the rejection of this separation in the course of the *Phenomenology* undermines the view that knowledge of things-in-themselves is impossible, and provides a justification of a philosophic science which claims to know things as they really are.

In the *Science of Logic* Hegel repeatedly confirms this interpretation of the *Phenomenology*'s major function:

> In the *Phenomenology of the Spirit* (Bamberg and Würzburg, 1807) I have presented the consciousness in its forward movement from its first immediate *opposition of itself and its object* all the way to absolute knowledge. This path goes through all forms of the relation of consciousness to its object and *has the concept of science as its result.* This concept requires therefore ... no justification here, because it has already received one there. This concept is incapable of any *justification* other than this production of it by consciousness, for consciousness resolves all its own forms in this concept as in the truth.[50]

50. *Logic*, 1:29 (my italics).

This justification is clearly associated with the removal of the subject-object distinction:

> The concept of pure science and the deduction of it are assumed in the present treatise inasmuch as the *Phenomenology of the Spirit* is *nothing other* than the deduction of it. Absolute knowledge is the truth of all modes of consciousness, because, as that development made clear, only in absolute knowledge has the separation of the object and the certainty of oneself completely resolved itself.[51]

It is concluded that pure science "presupposes liberation from the opposition of consciousness," which is later described as the opposition between an "independent subjective being and a second such being, an objective one."[52]

Although Hegel himself says that the *Phenomenology* is "nothing other than" the justification or deduction of science by means of the removal of the opposition between subject and object, he was well aware that the book contained an abundance of material which was not relevant to this end. In a section of the *Encyclopedia* which gives added support to this interpretation of the overall function of the *Phenomenology*,[53] he adds:

> It was impossible to restrict it to the formal aspects of bare consciousness, for the standpoint of philosophical

51. *Logic*, 1:30 (my italics).
52. *Logic*, 1:42. This passage repeats and reenforces the one on page 30.
53. Sec. 25. The introduction is seen as being necessary to combat the idea that thought is "only subjective and has an enduring opposite in the objective."

knowledge is at the same time the most concrete and richest in content. Arising as a result, it presupposed the concrete forms of consciousness, such as morals, ethics, art, and religion. In the development of what at first appears to be limited to the formal aspects of consciousness, there is at the same time the development of the content or objects of the special branches of philosophical science. . . . The presentation thereby becomes more complicated, and what belongs to the more concrete branches of philosophy is put, in part, into that introduction.[54]

Although Hegel confesses and tries to justify the inclusion of material extraneous to the major function of the *Phenomenology,* he in no way repudiates his general conception of the book. In fact, if he had not retained this conception, there would have been no need to justify these elements, which are extraneous only in relation to what he regarded to be the general function of the book.

TRUTH, FREEDOM, AND THE THING-IN-ITSELF

I argued in the first chapter that Hegel views all human endeavor as the varied expression of one basic drive, which encompasses both theoretical and practical endeavor, both attempts to know and attempts to act. But as the one goal of the basic drive Hegel seemed to offer two different things: truth and freedom. He gives the normally epistemological concept of truth an additional practical interpretation, and the normally practical concept of freedom an additional epistemological interpretation, giving each the practico-epistemological

54. *Enc.,* sec. 25.

duality requisite for the goal of this corresponding dual drive. But although each was made eligible, it still seemed that two candidates were being endorsed for one position.

I claimed that this apparent inconsistency was relieved by Hegel's identification of truth and freedom, but I was able to present only part of the mechanism of this identification. Hegel argued that freedom is found only in conceptual thought, because, since the objects of conceptual thinking are the subject's own thoughts, the subject does not rely on any external objects and thus becomes self-sufficient, autonomous, and independent.[55]

To complete the identification, truth also must be linked to the autonomy of conceptual thought, and thus to freedom. Then the concepts of truth and freedom will have been identified with each other by identifying each with the bridge concept of autonomy or self-sufficiency. The concept of autonomy is able to serve as a bridge between the normally practical concept of freedom and the normally epistemological concept of truth only because it is broad enough to be interpreted both epistemologically (as knowledge which requires no external object, i.e., self-knowledge) and practically (as independent action). If truth can be somehow linked and limited to self-knowledge, then it can be identified with freedom through the bridge concept of autonomy.

But why is autonomy, even in the epistemological sense, necessary for truth? In other words, why must genuine knowledge be, in some sense, self-knowledge? For Hegel, genuine knowledge has to be knowledge

55. See Chap. 1, "Stoicism."

of things as they really are in themselves, not merely knowledge of appearances. Since the opposition of the knowing subject and its object is held to be responsible for the limitation of knowledge to appearances, genuine knowledge is possible only where this opposition has been overcome. Only where knowledge has no external object, that is, where it is self-knowledge, is truth attainable. The spirit, in seeking truth, must seek autonomy, and to seek autonomy is to seek freedom; to seek freedom and truth is to have but one goal. Hegel's identification of truth and freedom is of a piece with his rejection of the limitation of knowledge to appearances.

HEGEL'S ARGUMENTS AGAINST THE LIMITATION OF KNOWLEDGE

The entire *Phenomenology*, by "deducing" a final form of consciousness in which the opposition of subject and object is overcome, removes the objection to knowledge of things as they are in themselves. But the entire *Phenomenology*, viewed as a single argument to this end, is a grotesque, unwieldy demonstration involving many steps, most of which are of dubious relevance and validity. In the *Science of Logic* and the *Enclyclopedia* Hegel offers more manageable and direct criticisms of the Kantian position.

Since the limitation of knowledge is the result of "a major viewpoint of the Critical Philosophy, that before one attempts to know God, the essence of things, etc., one must first investigate the capacity of knowledge itself, to see whether it is able to accomplish such tasks,"[56] Hegel attacks this viewpoint. He claims that

56. *Enc.*, sec. 10.

the plan to examine knowledge before using it is based on a false analogy with tools: "If one does not want to fool oneself with words, it is easy to see that other instruments can be investigated and criticized without using them in the particular work for which they are designed. But the investigation of knowledge can only be performed by an act of knowledge."[57] This so-called 'tool' can be investigated only cognitively.

In the *Phenomenology* Hegel had merely noted the uncritical acceptance of the tool metaphor. Now the metaphor is critically examined and an important disanalogy pointed out. Both the plan to examine knowledge before using it and the tool metaphor on which it rests are rejected simultaneously. The plan is not only based on an inappropriate metaphor, but is also internally inconsistent. Since knowledge must be used to examine knowledge, the plan to examine knowledge before using it is paradoxical. It amounts to "wanting to know before one knows" and is "just as absurd as the wise resolution of that scholastic who wanted to learn to swim before venturing into the water."[58]

Knowledge can be examined only in use; the analysis and criticism of certain concepts cannot precede but must accompany their use. Much the same point was neatly put by Otto Neurath and adopted by Willard Van Orman Quine as the motto of one of his books: "We are like sailors who must rebuild their ship on the open sea, without ever being able to take it apart in a dock and reconstruct it out of the best components."[59]

57. Ibid.
58. Ibid.
59. Neurath, "Protokollsätze," in *Erkenntnis*, 3:206 (my trans.); Quine, *Word and Object*.

Hegel, like Neurath and Quine, denies neither the need
for an examination of knowledge nor its possibility; he
denies only the possibility of a *preliminary* examination:
"Of course the forms of thought should not be used
unexamined, but the examination is already a knowing.
Therefore, the activity of the thought-forms and their
critique must be united in knowing."[60]

THE CONCEPT OF THE THING-IN-ITSELF

Hegel also directly examines and criticizes Kant's
notion of an unknowable thing-in-itself. The thing-in-
itself is not supposed to be "posited and determined by
the thinking self-consciousness"; it is supposed to "remain foreign and external to thought."[61] But as Hegel
points out, "it is easy to see that such an abstraction as
the thing-in-itself is itself only a product of thought."[62]
The thing-in-itself, which is opposed to concepts, is
really just another concept. We know this because the
thing-in-itself is an abstraction, and all abstractions are
concepts and thus products of thought.

If the abstract character of the thing-in-itself betrays
it to be only another concept, its completely abstract
character shows it to be a rather dubious concept: "The
thing-in-itself . . . expresses the object, as it is in abstraction from everything that it is in relation to consciousness, in abstraction from all determinations of feeling
and from all determinate thoughts about it. It is easy to
see what is left over—the *complete abstractum*, the total
void, determined only as *a beyond*; the negative of rep-

60. *Enc.*, sec. 41, Z1.
61. *Logic.*, 1:45.
62. Ibid.

resentation of feeling, of determinate thought, etc."[63]
Hegel suggests that the thing-in-itself is a suspiciously
vacuous concept. One cannot say what it *is*; one can
only say what it *is not*.

Essentially the same sort of criticism was used much
later by Gilbert Ryle to attack the Cartesian concept of
mind.[64] Ryle charged that the mind and mental pro-
cesses had been defined solely as the negations of their
physical counterparts, that minds were described only as
not in space, *not* in time, *not* subject to causal laws, and
so forth. Since Ryle considered this theory of mind a
"para-mechanical hypothesis," Hegel might be said to
have considered the *Ding-an-sich* theory a "para-phe-
nomenal hypothesis." In each case the philosopher is
attacking what he considers to be a spurious dualism,
created by the artificial introduction of a pseudoentity
whose entire conceptual content is to be the negative or
opposite of its counterpart.

Hegel also attacks the alleged unknowability of the
thing-in-itself.[65] He again asserts the thing-in-itself to
be a product of the abstracting process of thought, and
identifies its completely abstract character with the
equally undetermined, abstract concept of Kant's (and
Fichte's) nonphenomenal self, whose only characteristic, according to Hegel, is to be identical with itself.[66]

63. *Enc.*, sec. 44.
64. *The Concept of Mind*, chap. 1, "Descartes' Myth."
65. *Enc.*, sec. 44.
66. "Kant clumsily said that 'I' *accompany* all my representations, also
my feelings, desires, actions, etc. . . . But 'I' in the abstract, as such, is
the pure relation to itself, which is abstracted from representation, feeling
and from every condition, as from every particularity of nature, talent,
experience, etc." (*Enc.*, sec. 20.).

The thing-in-itself is only this vacuous self-identity (*leere Identität seiner selbst*) of the nonphenomenal ego externalized and viewed as an object. Hegel's argument is that both the thing-in-itself and the noumenal self amount to nothing more than bare self-identity. Thus, there is nothing more to knowing them than being acquainted with and understanding the simple concept of self-identity. Far from being impossible, this is rather common and easy.

A second, similar argument for the knowability of the thing-in-itself follows from its completely negative character. Since the thing-in-itself is defined solely as the negation of all phenomenal qualities, Hegel argues that its conceptual content amounts to nothing more than the abstract concept of negation. In this case, not only is negation a familiar and easily comprehended concept, but it is ironically also listed by Kant as one of the necessary and universal categories of the understanding. "The negative determination, which this abstract identity receives as an object, is also included among the Kantian categories and is just as well known as that vacuous identity. Hence, only with astonishment can one read the so often repeated dictum that one cannot know what the thing-in-itself is. There is nothing easier to know than this."[67]

It might be objected that Hegel cannot advance both arguments, for although the thing-in-itself may be reducible to self-identity or to negation, it cannot be reducible to both. Hegel does not discuss this difficulty here, but he no doubt considered abstract self-identity

67. *Enc.*, scc. 44.

to result from the negation of all conceptual content and thus to be roughly equivalent to negation. And he actually argues along these lines in the equation of *Being* and *Nothing* in the first transition of his *Logic*. Hegel offers two different formulations of what, for him, is basically the same analysis because he feels that each of them clearly illustrates the knowability of the thing-in-itself.

Hegel's criticism of the notion of an unknowable thing-in-itself should be distinguished from several different but similar and more usual criticisms which have been falsely attributed to him.[68] A standard criticism of Kant's philosophy is that although the categories of the understanding are not supposed to apply to things-in-themselves, the latter are said to exist and to be the causes of our sensations. This entails applying the categories of existence and causality to them. It is further argued that if we know that the things-in-themselves exist and are causes, we know something about them, and thus they are, at least to some extent, knowable.[69]

These arguments are like Hegel's reduction of the thing-in-itself to negation in showing certain categories of the understanding to be applicable to the thing-in-itself. But Hegel's position is much more radical. He asserts not only that the thing-in-itself is at least partially knowable, but that since it is nothing more than the concept of negation or self-identity, it is completely knowable. Moreover, Hegel simply never uses the argu-

68. See Walter Stace, *The Philosophy of Hegel*, pp. 43–49.
69. For a defense of Kant against these arguments see A. C. Ewing, *A Short Commentary on Kant's Critique of Pure Reason*, (1938), pp. 187–95.

ments from the attribution of existence or a causal character to the thing-in-itself.[70]

Hegel further criticizes Kant's theory by posing the dilemma that either the categories are applicable to things-in-themselves, or the categories cannot be applicable to the understanding. For if the categories are really applicable to the understanding, then the categories are applicable to it as it really is—as a thing-in-itself.

> The critique of the forms of the understanding has had the result that these forms have no applicability to things-in-themselves. . . . But if they are allowed to remain valid for the subjective reason and experience, then the critique has not changed them, but allows them to remain valid for the subject in the same way that they formerly would have been valid for the object. . . . If they cannot be determinations of the thing-in-itself, still less can they be determinations of the understanding, to which at least the dignity of a thing-in-itself should be allowed.[71]

Hegel is *not* arguing here that Kant's categories are the actual determinations of the understanding; on the contrary, he denies their adequacy. He is merely calling attention to what seems to be an inconsistency in Kant's philosophy.

70. Yet Hegel would probably have endorsed these criticisms. In a letter to Schelling he makes a similar criticism: "If substance and accidents are corollaries, then it would seem to me that the concept of substance would not be applicable to the absolute ego—only to the empirical ego" (in Kaufmann, p. 304).

71. *Logic,* 1:27.

3 ~ SUBJECTIVITY AND OBJECTIVITY

Among the unexamined ideas held responsible in the *Phenomenology* for the unjust limitations philosophers had placed upon human knowledge are "the objective and subjective."[1] In these terms the limitation which philosophers had placed upon human knowledge amounts to the assertion that knowledge is merely subjective and not objective. Although Hegel considered the assertion that knowledge is subjective to be often just another formulation of the assertion that there is no knowledge of things-in-themselves, he realized that the two doctrines, though closely connected, were distinct, and he rejected them both.

One obvious way to do away with the philosophical embarrassment of the unknowability of any object as it exists independent of the knowing subject, that is, as a thing-in-itself, is to adopt some form of subjective idealism which denies the existence of anything "objective" and asserts that all reality and all knowledge of reality is in some sense "subjective." In this manner one can deny the existence of an unknowable thing-in-itself by holding that all we know, and all there is, is subjective. This flight from the Kantian dilemma of not being able to know ultimate reality is different from that romantic acceptance of the inadequacy of reason and reliance on direct, nonconceptual intuition that Hegel criticizes in the preface to the *Phenomenology* and in the section titled "Immediate Knowledge" in the *Vorbegriff* to the *Encyclopedia*. The subjective idealist does not reject

1. PG, p. 65.

the adequacy of reason, but rather ascribes to it, and to the ultimate reality it successfully knows, a subjective character.

Although Hegel distinguishes post-Kantian idealism from post-Kantian romanticism, he finds both unacceptable. For Hegel, reason must be retained as the way to truth, but not at the cost of making both reason and truth subjective:

> Transcendental idealism, carried more consistently to its logical conclusion, recognized the emptiness of that ghost of the thing-in-itself which the Critical Philosophy left behind—this abstract shadow, divorced from all content—and had as its goal to destroy it completely. This philosophy also made a beginning of letting reason produce its own determinations out of itself. But the subjective attitude of this attempt did not allow it to be carried to completion.[2]

Since Hegel wanted to show that reason could know an ultimate and *objective* reality, he rejected the subjective idealism of Fichte as well as the romantic intuitionism of Jacobi.

Even Kant, in spite of his doctrine of the thing-in-itself, is classified as a subjective idealist because he held that thought is subjective.

> The Critical Philosophy . . . like the later idealism, gave, as previously mentioned, because of its fear of the object, an essentially subjective meaning to the logical determinations. In doing this, it remained burdened with the object it fled, and a thing-in-itself, an endless impulse, remains as a beyond.[3]

2. *Logic*, 1:28.
3. *Logic*, 1:32.

Kant is said to have argued that "the categories have their source in the unity of self-consciousness, and that, for this reason, knowledge, in fact, comprehends nothing objective by means of them."[4] Hegel concludes, "If only this aspect is considered, Kant's critique is merely a subjective (shallow) idealism."[5]

But Hegel considers more than this aspect of Kant's philosophy. He attempts a full-scale analysis of the concepts, "subjective" and "objective," in conjunction with a thorough examination of Kant's use of them.

The need for conceptual analysis is stressed throughout Hegel's philosophy and especially in the *Vorbegriff* to the *Encyclopedia*. A large part of Hegel's respect for Kant is due to Hegel's belief that Kant had at least to some extent, tried to examine the concepts used uncritically by his rationalist and empiricist predecessors:[6] "The Critical Philosophy subjects the worth of the concepts of the understanding used in metaphysics—and also in the other sciences and ordinary thought—to examination."[7] And the fact "that the determinations of the old metaphysics were subjected to examination" is "without a doubt an important step."[8]

But because Kant's analysis is limited to distinguishing what is subjective from what is objective, Hegel

4. *Enc.*, sec. 46.
5. *Ibid.*
6. "This metaphysics . . . examined neither the content and worth of the determinations of the understanding nor . . ." (*Enc.*, sec. 28). "Scientific empiricism . . . uses the metaphysical categories of matter, force, not to speak of unity, plurality, universality, infinity, etc. . . . and uses those categories and their relations in a fully uncritical and unconscious manner." (*Enc.*, sec. 38.)
7. *Enc.*, sec. 41.
8. *Enc.*, sec. 41, Z1.

finds it inadequate: "This critique, however, does not deal directly with the content and the specific mutual relationships of these determinations of thought, but only considers them with respect to the contrast between *subjectivity* and *objectivity*."[9] Hegel does not object to this question per se; he objects only to the pursuit of this question to the exclusion of all others. He also thinks that Kant's major critical tools, the concepts "subjective" and "objective" are themselves desperately in need of examination.

HEGEL'S ANALYSIS OF SUBJECTIVITY AND OBJECTIVITY

Hegel's analysis of "subjective" and "objective" is interlaced with his exposition of Kant.[10] Hegel explicitly derives the first sense of these terms from the "linguistic usage of ordinary life" (*Sprachgebrauch des gemeinen Lebens*). In this common view, what is "present outside of us and reaches us through perception" is objective. "Subjective" means belonging to the perceiving subject, and, correspondingly, "objective" means belonging to its external object. In this sense, thought is subjective. Kant, by arguing that substance, cause and effect, and so forth, are categories of the understanding, produced by the knowing subject rather than presented to it as external data, had denied that they are objective in this sense.

Yet Kant's argument for the subjectivity of sub-

9. *Enc.*, sec. 41. And in the second *Zusatz* to this section: "Kant's examination of the determinations of thought suffers in an essential way from the defect that they are not considered for their own sakes but only to learn whether they are subjective or objective."

10. The most thorough discussion is in *Enc.*, sec. 41, Z2, from which the following quotations are taken.

stance, cause and effect, etc. is accompanied by, and even depends upon, an assertion of their universality and necessity. Kant had argued that all human experience *must* be experience of substances connected by relations of cause and effect, and that this universality and necessity can be accounted for only if these features of experience are unvaryingly imposed by the subject on the data it receives from the external world rather than being features of the world as it exists independently of being perceived. Because of the universality and necessity of these "categories of the understanding" Kant had, according to Hegel, called them objective: "However, Kant nevertheless called thought—more precisely what is universal and necessary—*objective*, and what is only felt, *subjective*."[11] In this second sense, what is objective is contrasted not to the knowing or perceiving subject, but to what is "particular" and "accidental."

In contemporary English the presence of roughly the same two sets of meanings for "objective" and "subjective" creates a danger of equivocation and confusion. For instance, a popular, if misguided, way of arguing for the relativity of ethical and aesthetic evaluations depends upon sliding from the first to the second sense of "subjective" that Hegel distinguishes. From the unobjectionable and seemingly innocuous assertion that all evaluations are subjective in the sense that they arise in a subject, one can easily slide to the more problematic view that they are subjective in the sense that they are not amenable to intersubjective debate, confirmation, or criticism. All opinions, judgments, evaluations, and thoughts are subjective in the trivial sense

11. *Enc.*, sec. 41, Z2.

of being in some way ascribable to a personal subject. Yet there is still a question about the subjectivity or objectivity of judgments recognized as emanating from a personal subject. This is a question about their intersubjectivity, their independence from the caprice, carelessness, and prejudice of any particular subject or subjects.

Although Hegel, following Kant, links the second sense of objectivity with universality and necessity, not with intersubjectivity, this distinction between being independent of any subject at all and being independent of any particular subject is operative in Hegel's distinction between the two senses of "objective." The categories of the understanding, though originating in the thinking subject, are objective because they are claimed to be found in *every* thinking subject. This can be described as their universality and necessity, but it amounts to the fact that the categories of the understanding are not just characteristic of some particular knowing subjects, but of all: they are intersubjective. The second set of meanings for "subjective" and "objective" seems no less a part of ordinary usage than the first. It also seems quite distinct from the first.

Hegel defends Kant's use of "objective" in this second way, but not by appealing to "ordinary linguistic usage." Hegel claimed that Kant had introduced this second sense of these terms into the language and was responsible for whatever limited currency it enjoyed in more sophisticated circles:

The here mentioned determination of the distinction between the subjective and the objective, established by Kant, is found today in the linguistic usage of more

highly cultured consciousness. For example, it is de-
manded of the judgment of a work of art that it be objective and not subjective, and by this is understood that
it should not proceed from the particular feeling and
mood of the moment, but should keep in sight the universal view, grounded in the essence of art. In the same
sense, in a scientific undertaking an objective interest
can be distinguished from a subjective one.[12]

The second way to use the term is argued to be an
advance over the first, not merely an acceptable addition
to it. But it would be pointless to argue that one of
two sets of meanings for the same words is superior unless there is some shared function in respect to which
they can be compared and contrasted. It is hard to
imagine arguing the relative merits of using "fit" in
the sense of a sudden seizure and using "fit" in the
sense of appropriateness, since the contexts in which the
two meanings would furnish viable alternative interpretations are rare. In order to show that one of the two
sets of meanings for "objective" and "subjective" is superior, Hegel must show that both, though distinct
from each other, can serve as the answer to the same
question.

Indeed, Hegel's argument for the superiority of
Kant's usage relies on the implicit claim that the use
of "objective" in either sense serves to designate what is
independently real and enduring. Kant's use of "objective" is argued to be a superior way of designating
what the ordinary use of "objective" also tries to designate, and therefore to be an improvement *evolving from*

12. *Enc.*, sec. 41, Z2.

ordinary usage, not simply an unjustified departure from it.

> The previously mentioned linguistic usage [the ordinary one] appears to be turned topsy-turvy by this [Kantian usage], and Kant has therefore been accused of linguistic confusion, but with great injustice. The following is more nearly the case. To the common [*gemeinen*] consciousness the sensuously perceivable things which confront it (e.g. this animal, this star, etc.) appear to be what is independent and enduring. Thoughts, on the contrary seem not to be independent but dependent on something else. But in fact what is sensuously perceivable is what is really dependent and secondary, and thoughts are, on the contrary, what is truly independent and primitive [*das wahrhaft Selbständige und Primitive*]. In this sense Kant called what is contained in thought (what is universal and necessary) "objective," and, indeed, with complete justification.[13]

Since Kant's new use of these terms retains and better fulfills some of their previous functions, his revision is not merely the gratuitous introduction of ambiguity and linguistic confusion. Hegel suggests that the philosophic use of terms should be based upon their ordinary use.

But he also insists that "ordinary linguistic usage" should supply only the roots of philosophic usage. The German *gemein*, like the English *common*, means popular and general, but also vulgar and low. When Hegel refers to ordinary (*gemein*) usage or the consciousness it expresses, the deprecatory connotation is stressed.

13. Ibid.

Although Hegel emphasized the importance of considering ordinary usage, philosophy is supposed further to develop and refine it, not just to revert to it. These philosophic developments and refinements themselves take root in the language, though in the case at hand their growth seems limited to the "more highly cultured" circles. Hegel's general view is that philosophy is nourished by general liguistic usage and, in turn, nourishes it.

Yet there is a third sense of "subjective" and "objective" which stems from Kant's *Ding-an-sich* doctrine and counters his second sense by reaffirming the subjectivity of thought: "But furthermore the Kantian objectivity of thought is itself only subjective, since, according to Kant, thoughts, though universal and necessary determinations, are still only our thoughts and separated from the thing-in-itself by an impassable gulf. On the contrary, the true objectivity of thought lies in the fact that thoughts are not merely our thoughts, but at the same time the essence [*An-sich*]of things and of what is objective in general."[14] The concept of *independent reality* which linked the first two senses of "objective," is operative. Kant's denial of the applicability of the categories to the independent reality of things-in-themselves amounts to a denial of any true objectivity to them.

After locating both objective and subjective elements within experience and equating the objective element with the universal, necessary, a priori element, Kant had ultimately made both elements of experience sub-

14. Ibid.

jective in contrast to an unknowable, unthinkable, but objective thing-in-itself.

TWO KINDS OF UNIVERSALITY

Here, Hegel is content to conclude that their "threefold meaning" shows that: " 'Objective' and 'subjective' are comfortable and current expressions, which nevertheless easily lead to confusion."[15] Elsewhere, he tends to opt for the second meaning in defending the objectivity of thought. This defense relies on an extension of the Kantian assertion of the universality of the categories of the understanding, an extension which depends upon an equivocation and reveals Hegel's misinterpretation of Kant's position.

Kant's point about the universality and necessity of the categories amounted very roughly to the assertion that *every* human consciousness *must* experience according to the same basic conceptual scheme. This scheme, which involves Kant's table of the categories of the understanding, is claimed to be universal because it is used by every experiencing subject. If this were in fact true of Kant's categories, they would be objective in the sense of being intersubjectively valid.

Hegel wants to argue the much stronger and more general thesis that all thoughts, not just Kant's limited list of categories, are objective because universal. But the sort of universality which he plausibly attributes to all thoughts is different from the sort Kant attributed to the categories and, more important, not of a sort to support the claim that thought is objective.

15. Ibid.

In making the transition from "sense-certainty" to "perception," early in the *Phenomenology*, and in introducing the *Encyclopedia*, much is made of the abstract, general or universal character of our concepts and words: ". . . the determination or form of thought is the *universal*, that is, the abstract."[16]

Hegel argues for the universal or abstract character of *all* thoughts and concepts in two ways. First, he appeals to the results of introspection:

> The determinations offered here and in the immediately following sections are not to be taken as [mere] assertions and as my opinions [*Meinungen*] about thought. But, since no deduction or proof can be given in this preliminary way, these determinations might [instead] be considered as factual data. Thus, everyone who has thoughts and observes them in his consciousness should find empirically that they have the character of universality and also of the determinations to be mentioned subsequently. Of course, a previous cultivation of our powers of attention and abstraction is required for this observation of the facts of our consciousness and our ideas [*Vorstellungen*].[17]

Secondly, Hegel appeals to the nature of language, which, he held, mirrors the nature of thought: "Since language is the work of thought, nothing can be said in it that is not universal."[18] The argument consists of trying to show that all locutions, even those that

16. *Enc.* sec. 20.
17. Ibid.
18. Ibid.

seem to refer only to a particular individual, really function as universals, that is, apply equally and indifferently to each member of a class of individuals.

We may attempt to use language to pick out or to refer to some particular thing of which we are aware through the senses, but, according to Hegel, this attempt is doomed to fail. The particular thing may be described by using nouns and adjectives such as "rose" and "red," but "rose" refers indifferently to any one of those many things which are roses, and "red" refers indifferently to any one of those many things which are red. That such descriptive concepts function in our language as universals, not as names of individuals, seems so obvious to Hegel that he hardly bothers to mention or argue for their universality.[19] Instead, he concentrates on those locutions that seem specially designed to refer to individual things—those that seem to pose the greatest problems for his thesis.

One way of limiting the general reference of "rose" to a particular rose would be to prefix a demonstrative to the description, for example, "this rose." It seems that by means of the demonstrative—"this"—language can refer to particulars, so Hegel must ask: "What is the *this?*"[20] "This" is analyzed into "the double form of its being as the *now* and *here.*"[21] In other words, by saying "this rose" I am referring to the particular rose present to me here and now, not to roses in general. When a speaker tries to specify a particular by using

19. However, "If I say 'anger,' 'rose,' 'hope,' for example, they are all familiar to me through sensation, but I speak this content in a universal way, in the form of thought." (*Enc.*, sec. 24, Z1.)
20. *PG*, p. 81.
21. Ibid.

"this," he does so by referring to its spatiotemporal position in relation to his own.

But both "here" and "now" are correctly used by the same speaker or by different speakers at different times and places. Any point in time is *now*, and any point in space is *here*, for someone properly located. "Now" is a universal which refers indifferently to every possible instant. "Here" is a universal which refers to every possible place.

Hegel felt that the universal character of these words and concepts had been generally misunderstood: "To the question, What is *now*? we answer, for example, now is night."[22] By using "now" we intend to refer to a particular time, and this answer identifies "now" with its intended referent. But the possibility of referring to any time as "now," is, for Hegel, proof that any such particular reference, though intended, can never actually be made.

The mistake of identifying a universal with one of the several particulars to which it indifferently applies is illustrated by pointing out its application to other particulars: "We write this truth [that it is now night] down. A truth cannot lose anything by being written down, and just as little by our preserving and keeping it. If *now, this noon*, we look again at the truth we have written down, we would have to say that it has become stale. . . . *Now* maintains itself but as something which is not the night; in the same way it maintains itself against the day, which it now is, as something which is also not the day, or generally as something negative."[23]

22. Ibid.
23. Ibid.

Analogously: "*Here* is, for example, the tree. If I turn around, this truth has vanished and turned into its opposite. Here is not a tree but rather a house. *Here* does not vanish but endures while the house, tree, etc. vanish. *Here* is indifferent to its being a house or a tree."[24]

What is true of *here* and *now* is also true of *this*; depending upon the speaker's spatiotemporal location anything can be a "this." And what is true of *this* is true of *that*. Similarly, anything might be referred to as "the individual" or even "this individual." The very locutions with which we try to refer to individuals are themselves universals: "When I say, 'the individual,' 'this individual,' 'here,' 'now,' all of these are universals. Everything and anything is an individual and a this."[25]

Since the specific reference of demonstratives is relative to the speaker, one attempt to salvage the use of demonstratives to identify particulars would be to refer them back to the particular subject who is using them: "Now is day, because I see it; here is a tree, for the same reason. . . . *This I* sees the tree and asserts the tree to be here; *another I* sees, however, a house and asserts, not the tree, but the house to be here."[26] Every speaker, however, refers to himself as "I": "*I* is only a universal like *now, here,* or *this.* . . . When I say 'I, this individual I,' I really say [i.e., refer to] 'every I.' What I say applies to everyone; everyone is [i.e., can refer to himself as] this individual I."[27] "Similarly, in saying 'I,' I mean myself to the exclusion of all others. But what I say ap-

24. *PG*, p. 82.
25. *Enc.*, sec. 20.
26. *PG*, p. 83.
27. *PG*, pp. 83–84.

plies to everyone; everyone says 'I' and means himself to the exclusion of all others."[28] Again, Hegel argues, the attempt to refer to particulars breaks down.

There is still another linguistic device with which we seem to refer to particular individuals—proper names. When I mention "Berlin," "G. W. F. Hegel," or "Socrates," I seem to refer in each case to a particular thing and not to any one of a class of things. Surprisingly, Hegel does not even attempt to undermine the apparently individual reference of proper names. Considering his previous arguments one might expect him to have argued that often a proper name has been assigned to more than one particular and that theoretically all proper names could be assigned more than once. In addition to the Berlin in Prussia there is a Berlin, New Hampshire; many Greeks have been named "Socrates"; and even if there has never been another man named G. W. F. Hegel," there is nothing to prevent the use of this name in the future.

Not only does the putative particularity of proper names remain unassailed, but in these passages proper names are not even discussed as threats to the theory that language is universal and cannot successfully refer to particulars. This omission is, if not justified, at least partially accounted for by Hegel's attitude toward proper names which briefly emerges in other passages. In the preface to the *Phenomenology* Hegel criticizes sentences in which "God" is the subject and various predicates are attributed to him because, among other reasons, the subject "God" has no conceptual content or is only a name. He holds that proper names have no

28. *Enc.*, sec. 20.

conceptual content; in other words, that they are meaningless. In such sentences, "it is above all the name as name that designates the pure subject, the empty unit devoid of concept."[29]

In the *Logic* proper names are admitted to be exceptions to the otherwise universal character of language, yet the force of these exceptions is not removed by denying their particularity, but by denying their significance: "By using 'this' one intends to express something perfectly determinate. It is overlooked that language, as the work of the understanding, expresses only what is universal, except for the name of an individual object. However, the individual name is meaningless in the sense that it does not express a universal."[30]

Proper names, if indeed meaningless, do not pose a serious threat to Hegel's thesis that language expresses only what is universal, for language, although it contains proper names, can still be said to express nothing *meaningful* which is not also universal. It might be argued that the expression of meaningless names is only dubiously expression at all. To deny that proper names have meaning or are concepts is not implausible and has the advantage of calling attention to differences between proper names and other kinds of words.[31] However, the way in which the meaninglessness of

29. *PG*, p. 53.
30. *Logic*, 1:104–5.
31. A similar conclusion was reached by John Stuart Mill, who said, "A proper name is but an unmeaning mark . . ." (*A System of Logic*, chap. 2, sec. 5). More recent philosophers of language have also held that proper names have no meaning, e.g., Paul Ziff, *Semantic Analysis*, secs. 106 and 180.

proper names is supported in the passage just quoted introduces an objectionable circularity into Hegel's theory. The universal character of all the meaningful content in language is maintained only by asserting proper names to be meaningless, but proper names are only asserted to be "meaningless in the sense that [they do] not express a universal." The universal character of the meaningful content of language is maintained only by assuming it.

This *petitio principii* is slightly ameliorated by the fleeting suggestion of a separate reason for denying meaning to proper names. Hegel adds as an afterthought that "individual names can be assumed, bestowed, or even changed arbitrarily."[32] Although this germ of an idea is developed no further, it is an interesting suggestion. Anything can be given any conceivable name. Some names might seem strange or in some sense inappropriate; a boy might be named "Jane," or a child of either sex "Abracadabra." Yet, in assigning proper names one cannot be mistaken in the same straightforward sense as one can be in describing something. To name one's son "Jane" is merely peculiar, but to describe a window as "a horse" is mistaken. The complete interchangeability of proper names might be accounted for by arguing that all proper names have the same meaning—no meaning.

Let us temporarily forget the circulatory and incompleteness of Hegel's justification for the thesis that proper names have no meaning; let us suppose this thesis is correct. It still does not follow that proper names, though meaningless, cannot refer to particulars,

32. *Logic*, 1:105.

unless meaning and reference are equated. Indeed, Hegel's position is elusive because he does not distinguish between the question of what is the nature of the conceptual content of language and the question of what it is to which language can refer.

LANGUAGE AND "MEINUNG"

Throughout his discussion of the universal character of language Hegel sharply contrasts what we intend (*meinen*) to do with language and what the nature of language allows us to do. Simply to equate the German verb *meinen* with the English "to mean" is incorrect, and to translate the noun *Meinung* as "meaning" is worse.[33]

In English "to mean" can be a synonym either of "to signify" or of "to intend." Ambiguity is usually avoided because the presence of a personal grammatical subject generally indicates that the verb is synonymous with "to intend," and the absence of a personal subject indicates that the verb is synonymous with "to signify." "*Meinen*" can be synonymous with "to intend," but not with "to signify." Correspondingly, only persons— not words, concepts, propositions, theories, or behavior —can be the grammatical subjects of *meinen*. *Meinen* can also mean "to be of the opinion that," especially where opinion is contrasted with knowledge, that is, where it is unsupported.

A *Meinung* correspondingly belongs to a person, not to a word, concept, etc., and should be translated "opinion" rather than "meaning." In discussing *Mein-*

33. See Sir James Baillie's translation of the *Phenomenology*, 2d ed., pp. 152–53.

ungen Hegel is not discussing semantics but rather certain opinions which he holds to have no meaning or expression in language, and which therefore are sublinguistic and subsemantic.[34] The meaning of a word or concept is its *Bedeutung,* not its *Meinung.*

Since a *Meinung* is an opinion, *meinen* might be translated by the archaic verb "to opine" in order to retain a common root for both noun and verb. But to retain the morphological similarity of the German noun and verb is not an unalloyed virtue, for they differ semantically: although *Meinung* is never synonymous with *Absicht* (intention), *meinen* is sometimes synonymous with *beabsichtigen* (to intend). No single English verb can consistently be used to translate *meinen.*[35]

With the aid of a pun, Hegel further derogates *meinen* and *Meinungen* as being subjective in the sense of idiosyncratic: "What I merely opine (*Was ich nur meine*) is mine (*ist mein*), belongs to me as to this particular individual."[36] More disturbing than the casual use of a pun to make a point is the implicit confusion of different senses of subjectivity which Hegel himself distinguished. Certainly all my opinions, like all my thoughts, are mine in the trivial sense that I entertain them. They are subjective simply in being the opinions

34. In the *Enc.,* sec. 88, Hegel denies that there is any difference between two particular concepts by calling this difference "ineffable, mere opinion" (*das Unsagbare, die blosse Meinung*). *Enc.,* sec. 87; *Logic,* p. 77; *PG,* p. 88 also illustrate Hegel's attribution of ineffability to *Meinungen* and what we *meinen.*

35. I have evaded the problem in the following short quotations by using different words and indicating the occurrences of *meinen* in the original text.

36. *Enc.,* sec. 20.

and thoughts of an opining and thinking subject. But because my opinions are mine in this trivial sense, it does not follow that they cannot be shared by others, or that they are not amenable to intersubjective debate, confirmation, or criticism. To be mine is not necessarily to be only mine.

Hegel is trying to contrast opinions (*Meinungen*), which he claims to be particular and therefore inexpressible in language, with thoughts (*Gedanken*), which are universal and expressible: "If, however, language expresses only what is universal, I cannot say what I merely intend [*meine*]."[37] However, this fallacious argument for the idiosyncrasy and lack of intersubjectivity of *Meinungen* applies no less well to thoughts, for thoughts are subjective in the trivial sense of being the thoughts of some thinking subject. Yet thoughts are, according to Hegel, exactly what language can and does express.

The supposed lack of intersubjectivity which is held to render *meinen* particular and therefore inexpressible in language is not only ill argued but otiose. Our *Meinungen* are inexpressible for a different reason: according to Hegel, what we intend (*meinen*) is to refer to particulars, and, as we have seen, Hegel has independent arguments for the impossibility of linguistically referring to particulars.

This line of argument has further sweeping philosophic consequences. Since these particulars are presented to us in sensation and feeling, to deny the possibility of linguistically referring to particulars is also to deny the possibility of linguistically expressing what we

37. Ibid.

sense and feel. Hegel is thus attacking the foundation of any empiricism which views one of the most fundamental and unproblematic functions of language to be the reporting of the individual data of sensation.

For those of a certain mystical bent, what is ineffable is the highest, truest, and most real; the extralinguistic is the supralinguistic. For Hegel, on the contrary, ineffability is a defect; the extralinguistic is the sublinguistic: "And the *ineffable* [*das Unsagbare*] feeling and sensation is not the most excellent and true but the least important, the least true."[38] And "what is called the ineffable [das Unaussprechliche] is nothing but the untrue, irrational, the merely believed [*Gemeinte*]."[39] The excellence of the effable is not directly argued in these passages; it is simply stated.

It follows that we are to rejoice, not despair, that language does not allow the expression of the sensuous particulars which we intend to express. If what the "divine nature" of language rejects is shown to be unreal, untrue, and unimportant, then the possibility of linguistic expression serves as a welcome test of truth. Even in vainly attempting to express sensuous particulars, "I experience what the truth of sense-certainty, in fact, is . . . i.e., a universal."[40] An unsuccessful attempt to give linguistic expression to one of the forms of consciousness in the *Phenomenology* provides the nec-

38. Ibid.
39. *PG*, p. 88.
40. *PG*, p. 89. Also, p. 82—"Language is, as we see, the truer; in it we directly refute our *Meinung*. And since the universal is the truth of sense-certainty, and language expresses only this truth, it is impossible for us ever to express [*sagen*] a sensible being that we intend to express [*meinen*]."

essary impetus to *progress* to a higher form. For Hegel, the limits of language are laudable.

THREE PROBLEMS

Even if we accept Hegel's central conclusion that our mental concepts and their linguistic correlates—thoughts and words—are universals, three major problems remain. (1) From the conclusion that words are universals, does it follow that language cannot be used to refer to particulars? (2) From the conclusion that thoughts are universals, does it follow that thoughts are in any sense objective? (3) Does Hegel consider the universal to be truer than the particular only because the former but not the latter is expressible in language?

1. *From the conclusion that words are universals, does it follow that language cannot be used to refer to particulars?* Let us temporarily dismiss the possibility of referring to particulars by means of proper names. Even if the thoughts and words at our disposal are all universals, it does not follow that we cannot think or speak of a particular individual, for the following reasons:

First, although each of the thoughts or words used applies to a whole class of things, a complex enough combination of universals may apply to only one thing.

Second, as P. F. Strawson has elaborately argued, individuals can be referred to by supplying both their spatial and temporal positions.[41] This second way of

---

41. *Individuals*, esp. pp. 15–30. Strawson's theory, in stressing the importance of the spatiotemporal framework for referring to particulars, approaches Hegel's analysis of *this* into *here* and *now*. But, of course, in affirming the possibility of referring to particulars with language, Strawson radically differs from Hegel.

referring to individuals is really based on the first. The concepts of meridian, parallel, hour, minute, second, and the ordinal and cardinal numbers are all universals. Yet by combining them in various ways reference can be made to unique spatiotemporal positions. And by combining these unique spatiotemporal positions with descriptions we can refer to particular individuals. For example, we can refer unambiguously to this particular red chair by identifying it as the red chair at a numerically specified longitude, latitude, and date. Put in a more Hegelian manner, the use of a spatiotemporal framework to identify individuals shows that there is a way to specify any *this, here,* and *now* which "cannot lose anything by being written down and just as little by our preserving and keeping it."[42]

Third, although by assigning numerical spatial and temporal coordinates it is theoretically possible to refer to an individual in a way which can be recorded and preserved *salve veritate,* Hegel's arguments suggest that our ordinary attempts to refer to individuals by using demonstratives like "this," "here," and "now" are still failures. According to Hegel, only those statements are true which are still true when reread after being written down and kept for any length of time. It is also suggested, though not actually stated, that a true statement should still be true if reread after being written down and carried to another place or given to someone else to read. In short, according to this criterion the truth of a statement must be independent of its context of utterance.

A great many statements normally considered unob-

42. *PG,* p. 81.

jectionable do not pass this test, for example: "This is a book," "Now it is noon," "Here is the library," "I am happy," "The book is red," "He is intelligent." Whether these statements are true or false depends upon the context in which they are uttered—the speaker, the place, the time, etc. Either we must go along with Hegel and consider all these statements whose truth is not independent of their context of utterance to be automatically false, or we must reject Hegel's criterion for the truth of statements. The latter alternative seems much more sensible.

However, to reject Hegel's criterion only to consider all such statements automatically true would be equally ridiculous. Calling attention to the context-dependent nature of certain statements—as Hegel does—only makes clear the inadequacy of any theory—like Hegel's own—which does not make a distinction between statement types and statement tokens[43] and implies that truth and falsity apply to statement types, not to tokens.

W. V. O. Quine, for instance, is led to reject any such theory because of the very same considerations.

> Strictly speaking, what admits of truth and falsity are not statements as repeatable patterns of utterance, but individual events of statement and utterance. For utterances that sound alike can vary in meaning with the occasion of the utterance. This is not only due to careless ambiguities, but to systematic ambiguities which are essential to the nature of language. The pronoun "I" changes its reference with every change of speaker;

---

43. If "the rose is red" is uttered or written at one time and then uttered or written at another time or by another person, two tokens of the same type have been uttered or written.

"there" changes its reference with every significant
movement through space; and "now" changes its reference every time it is uttered.[44]

Hegel's discovery of the universal character of the
words with which we attempt to refer to particulars led
him to conclude that statements which purport to refer to particulars fail to do so and are false. Although
his discovery does not warrant his conclusion, it does
have important implications for any theory of linguistic
reference. Hegel's discussion of demonstratives shows
that any statement which refers to particulars by means
of them does not do so simply in virtue of a meaning
which it possesses as a statement type in abstraction
from the various contexts of its use. Such statements,
contrary to Hegel's conclusion, do refer to particulars,
but only as individual instances of repeatable patterns
of utterances, as tokens of types, used in specific linguistic and nonlinguistic contexts.

2. *From the conclusion that thoughts are universals,
does it follow that thoughts are in any sense objective?*
Hegel's discussion of language and reference is really
an outgrowth of what for him was a more crucial task.
Since language is "the work of thought," to show the
universal character of words serves to show the universal
character of the corresponding thoughts. And from the
universality of thoughts he wants to argue for their
objectivity. If thought is objective, knowledge of
thought—which Kant allowed—is not merely subjective
and limited. It becomes knowledge in the fullest sense,
and Kant's limitation on knowledge is removed.

Kant had argued that certain categories of the under-

44. *Methods of Logic*, p. xi.

standing were universal in the sense that every human consciousness uses them; he argued that the categories were objective in the sense of being intersubjectively valid. Hegel argues for the universality not only of Kant's twelve categories of the understanding but of all concepts. He seems to be arguing a much stronger thesis than Kant, but the two theses cannot be so simply compared because Hegel has not really argued for the universality of all concepts in the same sense that Kant argued for the universality of the categories.

Hegel, as we have seen, argues that all concepts are universals in the sense that they refer indifferently to any and all members of a certain class. But even if all the concepts people use are universals, that is, class concepts, there is no guarantee that all people use the same concepts to refer to the same classes. There is no guarantee that everyone uses the same system of universals in thinking. For example, the words "beautiful," "good," "democratic," and "philosophy" are all universals in the sense Hegel has argued. It is no less true that any one of these words and its corresponding concept can be and is in fact used and applied differently by different people. It is a commonplace that people disagree violently about what particular things are to be classified as "beautiful," what particular actions are to be classified as "good," and what particular institutions are to be classified as "democratic." The fact that our concepts are universals, and not names of particulars, does not imply that they are also universal in the sense that their use is intersubjectively consistent, or even that it is amenable to intersubjective confirmation and criticism.

If Kant's claim that the same basic categories of the

understanding are used by every human consciousness were true, then they would be objective in the sense of being true of all subjects, that is, intersubjective. But even if all thoughts are universals, they need not be objective in this sense. Hegel confuses something's being a universal with its being universally true of all subjects.

3. *Does Hegel consider the universal to be truer than the particular only because the former but not the latter is expressible in language?* It is clear that, for Hegel, what can be expressed in language is for that reason more excellent, real, and true than what cannot be so expressed, and that what language can express is the universal. However, the greater reality and truth of the universal is not only based on its being expressible in language but is reinforced by other arguments. The just criticized claim for the objectivity of the universal, which is based on a confusion between being a universal and being universally true, is one such putative reenforcement.

Additional support is mustered by trading on the traditional distinction between essence and accident. According to this view, the substance or reality of a thing resides in its essence or inner nature, that which remains the same through the vicissitudes of accidental change; what does not endure through change is only accidental. Individual things come to exist and cease to exist; individual animals are born and die. What endures through this change is obviously not the individual thing but the species to which it belongs. Therefore, it is argued, the species is the essence and reality, and the individual is only accidental. The species is identified with the universal, for the universal refers indifferently to each member of the species; "animal" refers indifferently to each thing that is an animal. It follows that the universal is the enduring essence and, therefore, more true and real than the particular.

A more specific example is that when we speak of a specific animal, we say, "it is [an] animal." We can point out a specific animal but not animal as such. Animal does not exist, but it is the universal nature of individual animals, and every existing animal is something much more concretely specific and special. But to be [an] animal, the species as the universal, belongs to the specific animal and constitutes its specific essentiality. If we subtracted from a dog its being an animal, it would be impossible to say what it was. Things in general have an enduring, inner nature and an external existence [*Dasein*]. They live and die, come to be and pass away; their essentiality, their universality is the species, and this is not to be understood merely as what they have in common.[45]

Hegel has identified thought with the universal. Thus in identifying the essence or inner nature of things with the universal, Hegel is identifying ultimate reality with thought and with what thought can grasp. Consequently, he is arguing against any denial that thought can know ultimate reality. He wants to show that the study of thought (the universal) and what thought can grasp is also the study of objective reality. Indeed Hegel adduces this traditional argument for the reality of the species in a *Zusatz* to support the position that

45. *Enc.*, sec 24, Z1.

"thoughts . . . can be called *objective* thoughts, including the forms which, to begin with, are considered in the ordinary logic to be only forms of conscious thinking. Logic [the science of thoughts] therefore coincides with metaphysics as the science of things grasped in thoughts, which are considered to express the essences of things in thought."[46]

46. *Enc.*, sec. 24.

PHILOSOPHY AND THE INFINITE

The view that philosophy attempts to attain an unrestricted or absolute knowledge is, for Hegel, tantamount to the view that philosophy attempts to know an absolute object or "the Absolute." The soundness of this identification is questionable[1] but unimportant, for Hegel supports the view that philosophy seeks to know the Absolute, not just by deriving it from the view that philosophy seeks absolute knowledge, but by appealing to history: "The history of philosophy is the history of the discovery of thoughts about the Absolute, which is its object."[2] In other words, he views philosophy as having been historically the search for a completely comprehensive and adequate metaphysics.

Hegel says not only that philosophy has "the Absolute" for its object, but also that it has "absolute objects."[3] He offers as examples the soul, the world, God, freedom, and spirit. But though these are indeed traditional philosophic concerns, why are they *absolute objects?*

Traditional metaphysical speculation about these objects had been criticized for being nonempirical by both the British empiricists and Kant: "In common with empiricism, the Critical Philosophy takes experience to be the only basis for knowledge."[4] Hegel agrees

1. The identification seems to rely on the unsound assumption that any knowledge must have an object to which can be ascribed all the characteristics ascribable to the knowledge itself. Crude knowledge is, for example, not necessarily knowledge of crude objects.
2. *Enc.*, Preface to the 2d ed., p. 10.
3. *Enc.*, sec. 10.
4. *Enc.*, sec. 40.

111

that these objects cannot be treated by any of the ordinary "empirical sciences," which take experience as their point of departure and then develop general laws and theories about it. However, the reason for this is not that these objects are not to be found in experience: "To be sure, they are not experienced through the senses, but whatever is in consciousness is experienced —this is even a tautology."[5] Rather, what puts these traditional philosophical objects beyond the reach of empirical science is that they "immediately present themselves as *infinite* [*unendlich*] in content."[6]

Hegel thought that he had deftly and conclusively countered the empiricist criticism that the objects of metaphysical speculation are not to be found in experience. Of course, he admits that they are not experienced through the senses, but suggests that this is also true of the general laws and theories produced by the empirical sciences.[7]

For Hegel, what seems to make traditional philosophical speculation peculiarly problematic is its attempt to know objects that are infinite. Furthermore, it is their infinite character that makes these objects "absolute." "Infinite" and "absolute" are used interchangeably. Hegel says that the "thought used in the philosophical way of knowing needs itself to be justified concerning . . . its ability to know absolute objects."[8] The need for such a justification is established in the immediately preceding paragraph: "What is usually

5. *Enc.*, sec. 8.
6. Ibid.
7. *Enc.*, sec. 7.
8. *Enc.*, sec. 10.

called a *concept* is to be distinguished from a concept in the speculative sense. It is in the former, one-sided sense that the assertion that the infinite could not be grasped by concepts is advanced, repeated thousands and thousands of times, and made into a prejudice."[9] The prejudice against conceptually grasping the infinite necessitates justifying the possibility of knowing the Absolute, for Hegel treats "infinite" and "absolute" as synonymous.

Hegel explicitly identifies these infinite and absolute objects as the objects of the pre-Kantian metaphysics,[10] and calls attention to Kant's attack on the metaphysical attempt to know them. Kant had considered metaphysical speculation to consist in an illicit extension of the categories of thought beyond their proper sphere of application. He had sharply distinguished the proper application of the categories to experience by the *understanding* (*Verstand*) from their improper or transcendent application beyond experience by *reason* (*Vernunft*).

UNDERSTANDING AND REASON

Hegel adopted and adapted Kant's distinction. Like Kant, he associated reason with metaphysical speculation, and understanding with less ambitious intellectual enterprises. But just as Hegel rejected the idea that the distinction between the objects of ordinary empirical inquiry and the objects of metaphysical speculation was that the former but not the latter were to be found in experience, he does not treat the distinction between

9. *Enc.*, sec. 9.
10. *Enc.*, sec. 30.

understanding and reason as depending upon whether or not the categories are applied to experience. Again, Hegel makes the distinction primarily in terms of infinity, not experience. Reason, but not understanding, has the infinite for its object.

Hegel acknowledges that this way of drawing the distinction is also derived from Kant: "Kant was the first to set forth distinctly the difference between understanding and reason. He defined the former as having the finite and conditioned for its object and the latter as having the infinite and unconditioned as its object."[11] Kant had held that reason requires, with respect to any judgment, to know the condition of that judgment, namely, the premise from which the judgment follows as a conclusion. Since the condition is itself a judgment, reason requires, in turn, to know its condition. Reason is not satisfied until the series is completed and knowledge obtained which is not conditioned by anything further. Reason seeks to know the completed series of conditions, the series of consequents and their grounds, of effects and their causes. Since this completed series of conditions is itself unconditioned, reason seeks to know the unconditioned. Since the series of conditions seems to be infinite, knowing the unconditioned is tantamount to knowing the infinite. Kant argues that an infinite series could never be experienced; he supports his contention that reason transcends experience by pointing to the unconditioned or infinite nature of its object. Kant also tries to show how traditional metaphysical concerns about the soul, the world, God, and

11. *Enc.*, sec. 45, Z.

freedom are all manifestations of reason's attempt to know the unconditioned or infinite.

Although Hegel rejects the Kantian claim that the objects of metaphysics are not to be found in experience, he accepts Kant's view that reason, in the service of metaphysics, seeks to know the unconditioned, and explicitly identifies the unconditioned (*das Unbedingte*) with the infinite (*das Unendliche*).[12]

Kant had declared knowledge of the unconditioned to be impossible and "criticized this application of the categories [of the understanding] to the unconditioned, that is, metaphysics."[13] Hegel considers this criticism and limitation of knowledge—in contrast to Kant's limitation of knowledge to phenomena and subjectivity —as "the second side of the critique of reason" which is "in itself more important than the first."[14] In order to rebut this limitation of knowledge to the finite and the corresponding criticism of metaphysics as the illicit attempt to know the unconditioned or infinite, Hegel had to show that the infinite could be known. He identifies the infinite with the truth[15] and thereby turns Kant's criticism into a challenge. The prejudice that the infinite cannot be conceptually grasped is thus made tantamount to the belief that the truth cannot be conceptually grasped. This prejudice had to be refuted, and reason, which claims to know the infinite, had to be defended.

12. *Enc.*, sec. 45.
13. *Enc.*, sec. 46.
14. Ibid.
15. *Enc.*, sec. 28, Z—"The truth is, however, what is in itself infinite." See also sec. 62 and *Logic*, 1:17.

It is to this end that Hegel *adapted* Kant's dichotomy between reason and understanding. Hegel identifies the Understanding with ordinary thought and its extension and refinement in the empirical sciences—and admits that it is unable to comprehend the infinite. This inability is explained by the understanding's use of categories which are meant to be opposites and contradictories of one another: "If the determinations of thought are encumbered with fixed opposites, i.e., if they are of a *finite* nature, then they are incommensurate with the truth, which is absolute [i.e., infinite] in and for itself. In this case the truth cannot enter into thought. Thought which brings forth only finite determinations and operates with them is called *understanding* (in the more exact sense of the word)."[16]

INFINITY AS TOTALITY

To characterize understanding as operating with concepts and categories which are mutually exclusive and to identify this operation with ordinary thought is not particularly puzzling. Consider, for example, *large* and *small*, *round* and *square*, *odd* and *even*. But why should the fact that our ordinary conceptual scheme contains mutually exclusive categories make it unfit for grasping the infinite? To answer this problem we must examine Hegel's notion of infinity.

For Hegel, "a finite being is one which relates itself to something *else*; it is a content which necessarily stands in relation to *other* content, to the whole world."[17] Following Spinoza, Hegel holds that *to be*

16. *Enc.*, sec. 25. Note the implicit equation of the absolute, the infinite, and the truth.

17. *Logic*, 1:71 (my italics).

finite is to be limited by something else.[18] From this view it follows that "the whole world" or universe is infinite, for since it includes everything, there can be nothing *else* left to limit it. Hegel would undoubtedly consider any cosmology positing a finite universe to be *conceptually* impossible.

Hegel holds not only that the whole (*das Ganze*) cannot be finite, but also that anything less than the whole must be finite. Any "being" that is less than the whole of being, any "content" that does not exhaust all content, "necessarily stands in relation" to what remains. And to stand in relation to something else is, in Hegel's view, to be limited by it and thus to be finite.

In denying the possibility of infinite proper parts Hegel again follows Spinoza.[19] More important, he also completes his identification of *infinity* with *totality*. Now the whole, and only the whole, is infinite. In the *Science of Logic*, Hegel rejects one notion of infinity because "it is not the whole [*das Ganze*], but only one side of it . . . It is thus the finite infinite."[20] In the *Encyclopedia*, the traditional objects of metaphysics, which Hegel characterizes as infinite, are also said to be "totalities" (*Totalitäten*).[21]

The Hegelian identification of infinity and totality is not only absent from the usual conception of infinity

18. Spinoza, *Ethics*, part 1, proposition 8. "[Substance] does not exist as finite, for (by Def. 2) it would be limited by something else of the same kind. . . ."

Definition 2, "A thing is called finite after its kind, when it can be limited by another thing of the same nature. . . ."

19. *Ethics*, part 1, proposition 13, note. ". . . and by a [proper] part of substance, nothing else can be understood than finite substance."

20. *Logic*, 1:33.

21. *Enc.*, sec. 30.

but is also in direct conflict with it. An infinite series is commonly defined as a series with no last number, and the natural numbers (1, 2, 3, 4 . . .) are often cited as a paradigm of such a series. But the series of the even natural numbers (2, 4, 6, 8 . . .) and the series of the odd natural numbers (1, 3, 5, 7 . . .) have no last members and, accordingly, are also infinite. Since the set of odd natural numbers and the class of even natural numbers are proper subsets of the class of natural numbers, they would not be considered infinite by Hegel. Yet they are generally taken to be infinite.

We can now see why Hegel asserts that the mutually exclusive categories—the "fixed opposites"—of the understanding cannot grasp the infinite. In a conceptual scheme composed of mutually exclusive categories the domain of each category is external to the domains of the others: each concept has a "content which necessarily stands in relation to other [conceptual] content." Given Hegel's view that to be related to something else is to be limited by it and thus to be finite, it follows that each concept is a set of mutually exclusive concepts is limited by the others and is thus finite. For example, if a number is odd, it cannot be even. Thus, in Hegel's view, *odd* would limit *even* and vice versa. Given Hegel's identification of infinity and totality, such concepts, each a discrete and proper part of its conceptual system, are finite and thus unable to grasp the infinite.

THE FAILURE OF TRADITIONAL METAPHYSICS

The understanding, which "tarries in finite thought-determinations, i.e., in still unresolved oppositions," is

said to have its "most distinct and proximate development" in "previous metaphysics as it was among us
before the Kantian philosophy."[22] Because traditional
metaphysics operates with the mutually exclusive categories of the understanding, it demands to know, with
respect to any of its objects (the world, God, the soul,
etc.) which *one* of a set of mutually exclusive categories
applies to it. Traditional metaphysics asks whether the
world is finite or infinite, simple or composite, and so
on,[23] and assumes that one and only one of any set of
putatively exclusive categories applies: "This is in general the strict *either—or*, and according to it, the world
is, for example, either finite or infinite but only one of
the two."[24]

Hegel terms this attitude "dogmatism": "This metaphysics became *dogmatism* because it had to assume, in
accordance with the nature of finite determination, that
of two opposed assertions . . . one must be true and the
other false."[25] And, "Dogmatism, in the narrower sense,
consists in holding fast to one-sided determinations of
the understanding to the exclusion of the opposed
[determinations]."[26]

Since the objects of traditional metaphysics were the
infinite objects of reason, the fact that "the thought of
the old metaphysics was finite thought" doomed this
metaphysics to failure: "But the objects of reason cannot be determined by such finite predicates, and the
endeavor to do this was the defect of the old meta-

22. *Enc.*, sec. 27.
23. *Enc.*, sec. 28.
24. *Enc.*, sec. 32, Z.
25. *Enc.*, sec. 32.
26. *Enc.*, sec. 32, Z.

physics."²⁷ The result was "merely understanding's view of reason's objects."²⁸

Hegel argues that no concept that has a fixed opposite and is thus only *one side* or a *part* of a conceptual scheme can adequately characterize the objects of metaphysics, which arc *totalities*: "The dogmatism of the metaphysics of the understanding [*Verstandesmetaphysik*] consists in holding fast to *one-sided* determinations of thought in their isolation; in contrast, [the proper method of] speculative philosophy contains the *principle of totality* and reveals itself by transcending the *one-sidedness* of the abstract determinations of the understanding."²⁹

Although Hegel finds in pre-Kantian metaphysics a paradigm of the futile attempt to grasp the infinite by means of finite concepts, he also thinks that there is a timeless tendency to make this mistake: "This metaphysics is something in the past, however, only in relation to the history of philosophy. In itself it is really always present—[it is] merely understanding's view of reason's objects."³⁰ Since our normal mode of thought is the understanding, we naturally, albeit futilely, tend to apply it to the infinite objects of metaphysics.

KANT'S CRITIQUE OF TRADITIONAL METAPHYSICS

Hegel thought that Kant had rightly called attention to the failure of traditional metaphysics but had not correctly located the reasons for this failure. [As we

27. *Enc.*, sec. 28, Z.
28. *Enc.*, sec. 27
29. *Enc.*, sec. 32, Z.
30. *Enc.*, sec. 27.

have seen, Hegel held that this failure resulted from
the use of rigidly opposed—i.e., finite—categories to
characterize infinite objects.]

Kant had approached and paved the way for this discovery in his discussion of the "Antinomies of Pure
Reason." He had argued that, with respect to certain
metaphysical inquiries about the world, each of two
apparently conflicting answers could be equally well
supported. As Hegel describes it, "In attempting to
know the unconditioned of the second object, the
world, reason becomes involved in *antinomies*, i.e., in
the assertion of two *opposed* propositions about the
same object, so that each of these propositions must be
asserted with the same necessity."[31]

Hegel hailed Kant's "Antinomies" as proof of the
inadequacy of the finite, rigidly opposed categories of
the understanding for metaphysical questions: "This
thought, that the contradiction which the determinations of the understanding spawn in what belongs to
reason [*am Vernünftigen*] is *essential* and *necessary*, is
to be regarded as one of the most profound and important advances of philosophy in recent times."[32] The law
of the understanding—that of any two putatively opposed concepts one and only one is true of any given
object—seemed to be contradicted by Kant's examination of metaphysical speculation about the world.
Hegel took Kant's antinomies as evidence for the more
general inadequacy of this law and of the understanding
when applied to *any* of the traditional objects of metaphysics.

31. *Enc.*, sec. 48.
32. *Enc.*, sec. 48.

The antinomies helped to inspire and support Hegel's contention that none of the traditional objects of metaphysics is characterized by one and only one category of a pair of putatively contradictory and exhaustive categories, but each "is essentially the one as well as the other, and thus neither the one nor the other —i.e., such determinations in their isolation are invalid."[33] The antinomies seemed to show that "one as well as the other" of two opposed categories could be predicated of each of the objects of metaphysics—in other words, that in metaphysical speculation the law of noncontradiction breaks down. Since Hegel held that the laws of noncontradiction and excluded middle were of a piece, the failure of the law of noncontradiction was tantamount to a failure of the law of excluded middle— to the case in which "neither one nor the other" of two opposed categories is predicable. And if, as Hegel thought, these laws are of a piece with the understanding's mutually exclusive, "isolated" categories, the failure of the laws is also an invalidation of such categories for metaphysics.

But in contrast to Hegel, Kant had not concluded from his discovery of the antinomies that these contradictions resulted from the misapplication of the *finite* categories of the understanding to the *infinite* objects of metaphysics. Hegel uses the antinomies to support the radical claim that, *according to the finite categories of the understanding,* the infinite objects of metaphysics (the world, the soul, God, etc.) *are* nests of contradictions. And thus, so much the worse for the categories of the understanding.

33. *Enc.*, sec. 32, Z.

While highly esteeming Kant's discovery of the antinomies, Hegel lamented the timidity of Kant's conclusions: "The profunditity of this point of view is
matched by the triviality of its resolution, which consists only in a tenderness for the things of the world.
It is not supposed to be the essential being [*Wesen*] of
the world, but *only* the thinking reason, the essential
being of the spirit, which has the blemish of contradiction in it."[34]

The antinomies seem to show that the world, the
ultimate metaphysical reality, is contradictory according to the categories and laws of the understanding.
Hegel thought that Kant, in attributing the genesis of
the antinomies to a misapplication of the categories of
the understanding beyond experience to things-in-
themselves, had been merely adhering to the generally
accepted strategy of saving *ultimate reality* from contradiction: "If the world of *appearance* displayed contradictions to the observing spirit, no one would have
anything against it."[35]

But Hegel argues that Kant's attempt to preserve
metaphysical consistency is ineffectual. Even if one
were justified in removing the contradiction from the
essential being (*Wesen*) of the world and relocating
it in thought—the essential being of the spirit—ultimate
reality (of the spirit) would still be beset with contradiction. It might be argued that contradiction is not
part of thought's essential reality because contradiction
arises only when, in metaphysical speculation, the categories of the understanding are misapplied beyond

34. *Enc.*, sec. 48.
35. Ibid.

experience. However, as Hegel points out, "It is of no help to say that reason becomes involved in contradiction *only* through the application of the categories [of the understanding beyond experience]. For it is also asserted that this application is necessary, and that reason has no determinations other than the categories."[36] If this application must be made, it and the contradiction it generates are part of the essential reality of thought. Kant's "tenderness for the things of the world" had not only obscured the significance of the antinomies, but had also failed in its aim to keep reality free from contradiction.

Hegel traces the antinomies and the attendant failure of traditional metaphysics to the opposed and hence finite nature of the categories of the understanding, and he rejects Kant's location of the trouble in the misapplication of these categories beyond experience to things-in-themselves.

Hegel also occasionally redescribes the Kantian limitation of the categories to the phenomenal world, the assertion of their subjectivity, as another form of the assertion of their finitude: "More accurately, the *finitude* of the determinations of thought is to be interpreted in two ways: first, that they are *only subjective* and remain in opposition to what is objective; second, that, in generally being limited contents, they remain

36. Ibid. In the *Prolegomena to Any Future Metaphysics*, 351–52, Kant says: "We cannot indeed, beyond all possible experience, form a definite concept of what things in themselves may be. Yet we are not at liberty to abstain entirely from inquiring into them; for experience never satisfies reason fully but, in answering questions, refers us further and further back and leaves us dissatisfied with regard to their complete solution" (Lewis White Beck translation).

in opposition to one another as well as to the Absolute."³⁷ In both cases, finitude is introduced by the
presence of a fixed opposition. An objective reality,
external and opposed to thought, limits thought, just
as categories, external and opposed to each other, limit
each other.³⁸

Thus redescribed, Kant's explanation of the failure
of traditional metaphysics in terms of the subjectivity
of the categories of the understanding becomes an explanation in terms of the finitude of these categories.
Kant can now be praised as Hegel's precursor, and
Kant's error comes to consist only in failing to recognize
both forms of finitude besetting the understanding.

> To the Critical Philosophy we owe the great negative
> service of having won acceptance for the conviction
> that the determinations of the understanding belong to
> [the realm of] finitude, and that the knowledge which
> operates within this realm does not attain the truth. But
> the one-sidedness of this philosophy consists in attribut-
> ing the finitude of those determinations of the under-
> standing to the fact that they belong merely to our
> subjective thinking for which the thing-in-itself is sup-
> posed to remain an absolute beyond [*Jenseits*]. In fact,
> the finitude of the determinations of the understanding
> does not lie [only] in their subjectivity. Rather, they are

37. *Enc.*, sec. 25.
38. In the *Logic* (1:17) the presence of still a third fixed opposition,
that between form and content, is said to make the "determinations of
thought" finite and thus unable to grasp the infinite truth: "For as mere
forms, as different from the content, they are taken to stand in a determination which brands them as finite and makes them unable to grasp the
truth which is infinite in itself."

finite in themselves, and their finitude should be shown to lie in themselves.[39]

It is important that, while the Kantian philosophy attributed the finitude of the categories only to the formal determination of their *subjectivity*, in this polemic the categories are discussed in detail, and the categories as such are recognized to be finite.[40]

When Hegel speaks of the categories' being finite "in themselves," he is referring to their being "limited contents . . . in opposition to one another," and he clearly considers this interpretation of their finitude to be the more profound and fruitful one.[41] Kant had subjected "the worth of the concepts of the understanding used in metaphysics—and also in the other sciences and ordinary thought—to examination"[42] and discovered their finitude .But he had missed the most important aspect of their finitude, their mutual opposition and limitation, because he "does not deal directly with the *content and mutual relationships* of these determinations of thought, but only considers them with respect to the contrast between subjectivity and objectivity."[43]

Both Kant and Hegel agree that the use of the categories of the understanding for metaphysical speculation is inevitably a failure. Since Kant takes these categories to constitute the only conceptual scheme we could possibly have, for him this failure marks the im-

39. *Enc.*, sec. 60, Z1. Since the actual wording of the *Zusätze* is not Hegel's, I have interpolated "only" to remove the contradiction between this *Zusatz* and the more reliable sec. 25 (see above pp. 124–25).

40. *Enc.*, sec. 62.

41. See quotation from *Enc.*, sec. 25, on pp. 124–25.

42. *Enc.*, sec. 41.

43. Ibid. (my italics).

possibility of metaphysics. Hegel, on the contrary, allows for the possibility of revising or replacing this scheme, and thus allows for the possibility of metaphysics.

Kant blames the failure of the metaphysics of the understanding (*Verstandesmetaphysik*) on the impossibly ambitious aims of *metaphysics*, while Hegel blames it on the inadequacy of the finite categories of the *understanding*. Given the failure of *Verstandesmetaphysik*, metaphysical pursuits need be rejected only if the understanding is uncritically accepted. And Hegel charges that Kant failed to examine the understanding critically: "The Kantian philosophy allows the categories and methods of ordinary knowledge to remain completely uncontested."[44]

JACOBI'S REJECTION OF CONCEPTUAL KNOWLEDGE

As we have seen, Hegel interprets Jacobi's philosophy of immediate knowledge and intuition as a response to Kant's limitation of conceptual knowledge to appearances.[45] He also interprets it as a response to the problem of knowing the infinite, given finite categories of thought. Before the Critical Philosophy,

> thought [*Denken*] was credited with stripping away the finitude from sensuous representations of the Absolute, according to the . . . prejudice of all times that one reaches the truth only through reflection [*Nachdenken*]. Now at last, . . . thought has been declared to perform *only* the activity of *making things finite*. In Supplement VII to the letters concerning Spinoza, Jacobi has presented this polemic most distinctly . . .

44. *Enc.*, sec. 60.
45. See Chap. 3, "Hegel's Analysis of Subjectivity and Objectivity."

and has used it in the fight against knowledge [*Erkennen*]. In this polemic, knowledge is considered only as knowledge of the finite, as a procedure in thought from *conditioned* to *conditioned*, along a series in which everything that conditions is also conditioned—by *conditioned conditions*. In accordance with this polemic, to explain or comprehend [*begreifen*] is to show something to be *mediated* by *another*, and all content is only *specific, dependent*, and *finite*. The infinite, truth, God, lies outside the mechanism of this context, to which knowledge is limited.[46]

Since Jacobi believed that all conceptual knowledge [*Erkennen*] used categories which were conditioned or "mediated" by their fixed opposites—and thus were finite and metaphysically ineffectual—he rejected conceptual knowledge in favor of direct intuition or "immediate knowledge."[47]

Like Kant and Hegel, Jacobi accepted the impossibility of grasping the infinite objects of metaphysics with finite categories. Like Hegel, but unlike Kant, he refused to limit knowledge to finite objects and thereby deny the possibility of metaphysical knowledge. But like Kant, and unlike Hegel, he accepted the finitude of all conceptual thought. Therefore Jacobi, unlike Hegel, was forced to find knowledge of the infinite outside conceptual thought.

THE MERITS OF THE UNDERSTANDING

Although Hegel considers the understanding's isolated, opposed, finite categories inadequate for meta-

46. *Enc.*, sec. 62.
47. *Enc.*, sec. 63.

physical speculation about infinite objects, he does not reject these categories *tout court*. He holds that infinite objects cannot be grasped by finite categories, but that finite objects not only can, but can only be grasped by finite categories. Juxtaposed to his criticism of the old metaphysics for trying to determine the objects of reason with finite predicates, we find: "To be sure, concerning finite things, it is the case that they must be determined by finite predicates. Here the activity of the understanding is in its proper place. The understanding, being itself finite, knows, however, only the nature of the finite."[48] And in arguing that "the laws of inference which really serve a major function of the understanding" are "unusable" for higher forms of truth, he admits that it is "unjust to disregard that they have their field of knowledge within which they must be valid."[49]

When McTaggart argues that Hegel shows the categories of the understanding to generate contradictions wherever they are applied, he disregards the important Hegelian distinction between the unobjectionable, and even necessary, application of finite categories to finite objects and their contradiction-generating misapplication to the infinite objects of metaphysics: "The examination of a certain category leads us to the conclusion that, *if we predicate it of any subject*, we are compelled by consistency to predicate of the same subject the contrary of that category."[50] McTaggart erroneously sug-

48. *Enc.*, sec. 28, Z.
49. *Logic*, 1:17–18.
50. *Studies in Hegelian Dialectic* (London, 1896), 2d ed., 1922, p. 1 (my italics).

gests that, for Hegel, all employment of these categories, even in ordinary nonphilosophical contexts, is illicit and that to employ them even in ordinary ways "we must contrive for a time to arrest the [contradiction-generating] dialectic movement."[51]

Hegel argues that the necessary function of the understanding, its peculiar virtue, is to make clear, precise categorizations and distinctions.

> First of all, the rights and merits of even that thought which belongs merely to the understanding [*dem bloß verständigen Denken*] must be conceded. They consist in the fact that without the understanding neither constancy nor precision is attained in either the theoretical or practical realms. First, in theory, knowledge begins by comprehending the objects present to it according to their precise differences. In the study of nature for example, matter, forces, genera, etc., are differentiated, and each is fixed in its isolation.[52]

Because the categories of the understanding are not infinite, they are not sufficient for philosophy. But because only they are definite, they are necessary for philosophy: "After the preceding exposition, the fact that finally even philosophy is unable to do without the understanding scarcely requires to be specially mentioned. The most crucial thing for philosophizing is that every thought is comprehended in its full precision, and that one does not rest satisfied with anything vague or indeterminate."[53]

51. Ibid., p. 11.
52. *Enc.*, sec. 80, Z.
53. Ibid.

Since only the understanding can make precise categorizations and distinctions, to reserve it no role in philosophy is to abandon philosophy to feeling and intuition. In the *Vorbegriff* to the *Encyclopedia* this abandonment of conceptual thought is discussed as the "Third Attitude of Thought to Objectivity" and exemplified by Jacobi's philosophy. There, Hegel presents the view as a natural but unsatisfactory response to Kant's limitations of knowledge to appearances and to finite objects.[54]

Earlier, in the preface to the *Phenomenology*, both the popularity and unacceptability of the view that "the Absolute is not supposed to be grasped conceptually [*begriffen*] but felt and intuited,"[55] had been major themes. There, rather than explicitly identifying the view with Jacobi or any other figure, Hegel presents it as a general tendency of the time, as "a notion and its consequences that are as presumptuous as they are *widely accepted* in our times."[56] And rather than sympathetically tracing the motivation and genesis of this view, Hegel devotes his energies to a polemic against it.[57]

In this attack on intuitionist philosophy Hegel elab-

54. See above, pp. 64–66, 127–28.
55. *PG*, p. 13. Hegel also refers to it as the view that "the truth exists only *in*, or rather only *as*, that which is sometimes called intuition, sometimes immediate knowledge of the Absolute, religion, or being" (p. 12).
56. *PG*, p. 12. (Kaufman's translation, p. 374, my italics). Lasson suggests that Hegel was referring to "Jacobi, the romantics, Schlegel, and Schleiermacher."
57. However, in the following sentence Hegel adumbrates the clearer *Encyclopedia* presentation of the view as a response to the problem of knowing the infinite: "This prophetic talk . . . glances scornfully at determinateness (the *Horos*) and intentionally keeps its distance from the concept and from necessity—identifying these with reflection, which dwells in finitude" (*PG*, p. 15).

orately argues the indispensability of the understanding for philosophy. First, since the "analysis" of a notion involves differentiating its elements, and "the activity of differentiation [*Scheidens*] is the strength and work of the understanding,"[58] only the understanding can analyze our ordinary, subphilosophic notions and sensuous representations (our *Vorstellungen*). Hegel enthusisastically praises the understanding's capacity for analysis as "the most amazing and greatest, or rather the absolute power" and as "the enormous power of the negative."[59]

Second, Hegel associates the understanding (*Verstand*) with general intelligibility (*Verständlichkeit*), that is, with public accessibility. He argues that with the removal of the understanding's analyses, categorizations, and distinctions, philosophical truth becomes esoteric in the objectionable sense that no amount of intelligence and effort necessarily provide access to it. He laments the lack of the understanding's "development of the form whereby distinctions are determined with certainty and ordered in firm relationships," and then laments the consequences: "Without this development, science sacrifices general intelligibility and has the appearance of being an esoteric possession of a few individuals. . . . Only what is completely determined is also exoteric, comprehensible [*begreiflich*], and capable of being learned, and thus the possession of all."[60] Hegel is not merely trading on the similarity of *Verstand* and

58. *PG*, p. 29.
59. Ibid.
60. *PG*, p. 16.

Verständlichkeit. If philosophical truth is revealed only by a special intuition which not all men possess, this truth is, indeed, esoteric and not publicly accessible.

Hegel is well aware that the intellectual demands of philosophy are too rigorous for most people. Analysis requires "the seriousness, pain, patience, and work of the negative."[61] Trying to operate in the philosophical realm of abstract concepts (*Begriffe*) rather than with the usual notions and sensuous images (*Vorstellungen*) is, like "the attempt to walk on one's head," unusual, difficult and seemingly unnecessary.[62] But while Hegel finds it acceptable and predictable that philosophical truth be inaccessible to sloth and stupidity, he rejects any view on which philosophical truth may remain inaccessible to effort and intelligence.

Although reason (*Vernunft*), the mode of thought appropriate to philosophy, is different from understanding (*Verstand*), the ordinary mode of thought common to all, we must be able to reach reason through the understanding if philosophy is to be accessible to all: "The intelligible [*verständige*] form of [philosophical] science[63] is the path to science which is offered to all and made equal for all. To reach rational knowledge [*zum vernünftigen Wissen*] through the understanding is the justified demand of the consciousness that approaches science. For the understanding is thinking, the pure ego; and the intelligible [*das Verständige*] is that which is already known and common to both science and un-

61. *PG*, p. 20.
62. *PG*, p. 25.
63. In this passage, "science" refers to scientific philosophy, not the natural sciences.

scientific consciousness—that whereby unscientific consciousness can immediately enter science."[64]

DILEMMA AND DIALECTIC

Hegel is faced with a dilemma: the determinate and finite categories of the understanding are both indispensable and unfit for philosophic knowledge of the infinite. He must, therefore, develop a method of philosophic thought which somehow retains the fixed distinctions and oppositions necessary for conceptually determining an object, and also transcends the finitude inherent in such distinctions and oppositions. In philosophical reason, which seeks to know the infinite, the understanding's finite categories must be both preserved and negated—or, to use a term favored by Hegel just because it possesses this double meaning, *aufgehoben*.[65] If, like Kant, we simply preserve these categories, reason becomes an illicit application of finite categories to the infinite. If, like Jacobi, we simply negate them, reason becomes mere intuition or belief.

This dilemma is one important source of the method Hegel uses in the *Science of Logic* and in the shorter *Encyclopedia* version of this logic. This method, the famous *dialectic*, consists in examining the understanding's pairs of putatively opposed categories and showing that these categories, ordinarily thought to be mutually exclusive, really involve each other. They are shown to be one-sided abstractions from a concrete whole to which each belongs. Kaufmann rightly says, "That is

64. *PG*, p. 17.
65. "*Aufheben* exhibits its true double meaning . . . it negates and preserves at the same time" (*PG*, p. 90). See also, *Logic* 1:93–95.

the heart of Hegel's *Logic*; that is the meaning of its much misunderstood dialectic."[66]

However, it is not yet obvious how this dialectical analysis of categories is in part a response to the dilemma posed by the metaphysical task of knowing the infinite and the necessity of using the determinate but finite categories of the understanding for this task. I shall try to make this more apparent.

ANALYSIS AND METAPHYSICS

First, what does the analysis of categories, whether dialectical or not, have to do with traditional metaphysical speculations about the nature of ultimate reality? In introducing the *Science of Logic*, Hegel laments at length "the remarkable spectacle of a cultured people without a metaphysics."[67] And in the *Vorbegriff* to the *Encyclopedia*, he promises to remedy this situation in a logic which "coincides with metaphysics."[68] How does the analysis of categories in the *Logic* coincide with metaphysics?

Kaufmann's answer is that Hegel simply replaced traditional metaphysical speculation with conceptual analysis.

> With Hegel, metaphysics ceases to be speculation about the nature of ultimate reality. He is fond of speaking of 'speculation' and 'speculative,' but as a matter of fact *he does not speculate about things of which we could say that the time for speculation is long past because we now look to the sciences for verifiable hypothe-*

66. Kaufmann, p. 194.
67. *Logic*, 1:4.
68. *Enc.*, sec. 24.

ses. With Hegel, analysis of categories replaces speculative metaphysics. He gives metaphysics the new meaning and content that it still retains with some of the best philosophers of the twentieth century.[69]

Kaufmann's answer has two virtues: it rightly calls attention to the often ignored predominance of conceptual analysis in Hegel's *Logic*, and it also rightly denies the unwarranted charge that Hegel was vainly and anachronistically competing with the natural sciences. However, to cease competing with the natural sciences and to engage in the analysis of categories is *not* necessarily to abandon the traditional metaphysical quest for knowledge of ultimate reality

Hegel thought that metaphysics should not try to compete with the natural sciences, but not because he thought that the natural sciences had usurped the traditional metaphysical task of speculating about the nature of ultimate reality. Natural science could usurp the place of traditional metaphysics only if both had the same task, and for Hegel they do not. He holds that the natural sciences, which use the finite categories of the understanding, are adequate to their particular task of knowing ordinary finite objects, while traditional metaphysics has the different task of knowing absolute or *infinite* objects.

This traditional metaphysical task is still the task of Hegel's *Logic*. Hegel rejects the traditional means of metaphysics (the finite categories of the understanding), but only because he retains its end—knowledge of the infinite, absolute, "ultimate" reality of the world, God, the soul, and freedom.

69. Kaufmann, pp. 195–96.

The analysis of categories in Hegel's *Logic* does not replace speculative metaphysics; this analysis *is in the service of* speculative metaphysics; or rather, it *is* speculative metaphysics.

In the Introduction to the *Science of Logic*, Hegel describes his *Logic* as "the account of God, as he is in his eternal essence before the creation of nature and any finite spirit."[70] Kaufmann calls this "perhaps the maddest image in all of Hegel's writing"[71] and sensibly rejects its suggestion that the *Logic* takes us back to a time before the creation of the world. However, what concerns us here is simply Hegel's conception of his *Logic* as "the account of God" and his removal of it from the sphere of the "finite."

This passage is echoed and somewhat clarified at the beginning of the *Encyclopedia* version of the *Logic*: "Being itself, the following determinations of being, and logical determinations in general can be viewed as definitions of the Absolute, as metaphysical definitions of God."[72]

The *Encyclopedia* passage makes clear that Hegel is using "God" as an alternative theological idiom for absolute metaphysical reality, much in the way that Spinoza did. It shows that Hegel views his *Logic* not simply as an examination of categories, but as an examination of categories with respect to their adequacy as characterizations or definitions of the absolute, infinite, ultimate reality of traditional metaphysics.

This conception of the *Logic* is further reenforced

70. *Logic*, 1:31 (Kaufmann's trans., p. 195).
71. Kaufmann, p. 195.
72. *Enc.*, sec. 85.

by Hegel's historical parallels. He associates each of the first three categories of the *Logic* (*being, nothing,* and *becoming*) with a historical view which attempts to use that particular category as a *complete characterization of ultimate reality:* "First the Eleatics, especially Parmenides, pronounced the simple thought of pure being to be the absolute and the one truth. . . . It is well known that in oriental systems nothingness, the void, is the absolute principle. In opposition to those one-sided and simple abstractions the profound Heracleitos stressed the higher, total concept of becoming, and said that . . . becoming is all."[73] The examination of each of these categories is associated with the historical attempt to define absolute reality solely by means of it.

DIALECTIC AND METAPHYSICS

But even if Hegel's analysis of categories is addressed to the traditional metaphysical task of characterizing ultimate reality, how is the *dialectical form* of Hegel's analysis relevant to this task? More precisely, how is the dialectic a response to the dilemma posed by the task of knowing absolute reality, which is infinite, and the necessity of using for this task the determinate but finite categories of the understanding?

The finitude of a category, and thus its inadequacy as a definition or characterization of the Absolute, which is infinite, consists in the category's having a fixed opposite, which limits it. For example, *being* is usually opposed by *nothing, immediate* by *mediate, something* by *something else* . . . (*Etwas* by *ein Anderes*), *finite* by *infinite.* Although the pattern of Hegel's dialectical

73. *Logic*, 1:68.

analysis changes from case to case, it repeatedly attempts to argue that categories which are ordinarily thought to be mutually exclusive opposites actually involve each other. Putatively opposed categories are shown to be actually one-sided abstractions from a concrete whole of which each is only a partial aspect.

But a category that is or describes only a partial aspect of the reality of the concrete whole from which it is abstracted cannot be an adequate definition of this whole. An adequate definition of a concrete whole must include all its partial aspects. Thus, a definition is required which includes categories ordinarily considered to be mutually exclusive—a definition that not only includes these finite, one-sided abstractions, but also removes their specious incompatibility. This is accomplished by introducing as a definition a more concrete category that contains these abstractions as necessary elements. For example, the first pair of categories in the *Logic*, *being* and *nothing*, are argued to be abstractions which, contrary to ordinary opinion, do not exclude each other, and they are superseded by *becoming*, which is called "the unity of being and nothing."[74]

The dialectic *preserves* pairs of putatively opposed categories as the necessary elements (*Momente*) of more concrete categories. But as necessary elements of a more concrete category their mutually exclusive character is removed or negated. These categories are both preserved and negated—they are *aufgehoben.*

---

74. The analysis of the categories *finite* and *infinite* furnishes another example of this pattern. See below, pp. 141–46. Although this pattern is repeatedly used, far from all the *Logic's* analyses follow it. It represents Hegel's *initial conception* and *ideal* of dialectical form, from which his actual analyses diverge more and more in the course of the *Logic*.

Since for Hegel the finitude of a category consists in its being excluded and thus limited by an opposed category, the removal of the mutually exclusive character of categories by the dialectic is also the removal of their finitude. Thus, the dialectic is, at least in part, a philosophic method addressed to the dilemma posed by the necessity of using the finite categories of the understanding to comprehend the infinite reality of metaphysics. The dialectic resolves this dilemma by retaining these categories while removing their finitude.

If we ignore Hegel's description of his *Logic* as the analysis of various definitions of the absolute or infinite reality of traditional metaphysics, if we ignore Hegel's insistence that the traditional search for an adequate definition of this absolute reality is still *the* philosophic task, if we view his *Logic* as merely conceptual analysis and clarification for its own sake, we cannot account as well for the *dialectical form* of this analysis, that is, for its repeated denial of the putatively opposed character of various pairs of concepts. If we ignore the traditional metaphysical motivations of Hegel's dialectic, we make it more contemporary, but only at the cost of making it less comprehensible.

The *Logic* develops by repeating, albeit in a complicated and irregular way, this dialectical pattern. Categories in which speciously incompatible abstractions are preserved as compatible and necessary elements are themselves preserved and reconciled with their putative opposites in even more concrete categories. The *Logic*, at least in its general conception, is supposed to present a series of progressively more adequate characterizations of absolute reality. Hegel says that each category subsequent to *being* and *nothing* "is to be viewed only as a *more precise determination* and *truer definition* of the Absolute."[75]

Since the infinity of the Absolute is a presupposition of the *Logic* and a motivation of its method, it is not surprising that in the *Logic* itself *infinity* is one of the categories considered as a definition of the absolute: "Infinity as a simple concept can be viewed to begin with, as a new definition of the Absolute."[76]

But although Hegel insists that absolute reality is infinite, he also insists that this reality cannot be adequately defined by the concept of infinity as it is ordinarily understood. Ordinarily *finite* and *infinite* are held to be mutually exclusive opposites; ordinarily infinity is held to be "the negation of something else, of the finite."[77] But, paradoxically, *infinity*, like any other concept, is finite if excluded and limited by an opposing concept: "The infinite thus delineated is one of a pair, but as only one of a pair it is itself finite. It is not the whole but only one side of the whole; it has its limit in what is opposed to it; thus it is the finite infinite."[78] Hegel calls this finite infinite "the bad infinite, the infinite of the understanding."[79] It is the infinite, but "not yet in its final truth."[80]

As with the earlier categories of being, nothing, and

75. *Enc.*, sec. 87.
76. *Logic*, 1:125.
77. *Logic*, 1:127.
78. *Logic*, 1:133.
79. *Logic*, 1:128. See also p. 125.
80. *Logic*, 1:135.

becoming, Hegel associates the category of the bad infinite with an entire metaphysics based upon it. The conceptual scheme in which the (bad) infinite is separated from the finite is identified with a metaphysics in which "there are two worlds, an infinite and a finite."[81] There is the finite world that we presently occupy, a *Diesseits*, and an infinite world beyond it, a *Jenseits*. The infinite world is "separated from" (*abgesondert*) and "placed over" the finite world, and each "is given a different place."[82]

No names are mentioned, but Hegel's language strongly echoes his discussion of Kant's notion of the thing-in-itself, his discussion of Kant's ethical theory in the section of the *Phenomenology* titled "Morality," and his discussion of the Christian world view in the section of the *Phenomenology* titled "The Unhappy Consciousness." In Hegel's philosophy the concept of a *Jenseits*, a beyond, is the leitmotiv which links Kant, Christianity, and the concept of the bad infinite.

Elsewhere, Hegel says that Kant's thing-in-itself is "simply something beyond thought" (*schlechthin ein Jenseits des Denkens*)[83] and is "determined only as a beyond" (*bestimmt nur noch als Jenseits*).[84] Here, he describes the metaphysics of the bad infinite as containing: "the finite as the determinate being of this present place and time [*das hiesige Dasein*] and the infinite, which, though taken to be the *in-itself* of the finite, is nevertheless a beyond [*ein Jenseits*] in the dim,

81. *Logic*, 1:128.
82. Ibid.
83. *Logic*, 1:25.
84. *Enc.*, sec. 44.

unreachable distance outside which the finite is located and remains."[85] In this passage, Hegel not only characterizes the bad infinite, like Kant's thing-in-itself, as a *Jenseits*, but also directly links the bad infinite with the thing-in-itself.

In the section of the *Phenomenology* titled "Morality," Hegel argues that Kant's ethical theory, because it depends heavily upon the postulation of a second noumenal world of things-in-themselves in addition to the ordinary phenomenal world of our experience, depends in an objectionable way on a world which is essentially a *Jenseits*. He argues that, since for Kant an action is moral only when it results from duty prevailing against sensual inclination, the removal of the conflict between sensual inclination and morality is paradoxically the removal of moral action. "This moral consummation in which the battle betwen morality and sensuality has ceased," "this harmony of morality and sensuality," is also the destruction of morality and thus cannot be allowed to occur, to become "present." For this reason, moral consummation is "dishonestly displaced . . . beyond [*jenseits*] consciousness at a foggy distance at which nothing can be precisely distinguished or comprehended."[86]

Hegel thinks that the noumenal world functions in Kant's ethical theory as a ruse, as an infinitely remote repository for the fulfillment of a morality which is em-

85. *Logic*, 1:128.
86. *PG*, pp. 438–39. Hegel typically turns ambiguity to his advantage. *Verstellen* can mean either to *displace* or to *dissemble*. As he did with *aufheben*, Hegel utilizes the several connotations of *verstellen* simultaneously. I have attempted to retain the dual connotation by translating *verstellen* as to *displace dishonestly*.

barrassingly also the annihilation of that morality. Since this world is essentially a *Jenseits*, by definition it is never present but always *beyond* the place and time at which we are. It is like *tomorrow* in the sense in which tomorrow never comes. To place an event in this world is merely a devious way of postponing it indefinitely.

> Therefore, this consummation is only a dishonest displacement of the matter, for morality would, in fact, abandon itself in this consummation, for morality is only consciousness of the absolute purpose as the purpose in opposition to all other purposes. Thus, morality is the *activity* of this pure purpose—conscious of the interference of sensuality, of its battle with and opposition to sensuality, and of lifting itself above sensuality. That this consciousness is not serious about moral consummation is immediately made clear when it dishonestly displaces this consummation to infinity, i.e., asserts that morality is never consummated.[87]

Hegel, in his discussion of the "Unhappy Consciousness," characterizes the Christian idea of an afterlife much in the same way that he characterizes Kant's noumenal world. In this afterlife, ordinarily referred to in German as *Jenseits*, goals frustrated on earth are supposed to be fulfilled. But because it is by definition an "unreachable beyond [*das unerreichbare Jenseits*], which flees, or rather has already fled, every attempt to grasp it,"[88] the hope it offers is spurious: "Where it is sought it cannot be found, because it is supposed to be

87. *PG*, p. 439.
88. *PG*, p. 164. In the *Logic* the bad infinite is described as an "empty flight" (1:135) and as "the Unreachable" which is "supposed to be unreachable" (1:138).

a beyond, the kind of thing which cannot be found."[89]
Christian afterlife offers the false promise of reward in a
tomorrow which by definition is always one day distant.

Hegel considers the bad infinite, Kant's noumenal
world of things-in-themselves, and the Christian afterlife each to be essentially a *Jenseits,* and he treats the
Kantian and Christian cosmologies as variants of the
same basic metaphysic of the bad infinite, in which
there are two worlds. He rejects the bad infinite as a
definition of the absolute and infinite reality of metaphysics because it is only a finite infinite. But this rejection is reenforced by his distaste for what he takes to
be self-deception and even dishonesty in both the
Christian and Kantian postulations of a transcendent
world. Even as Hegel rejects the bad infinite, he insists
on the great philosophical importance of finding a true
infinite: "*What alone matters* is not to take for the
infinite that which by its very determination is made
into something particular and finite. For this reason
we here directed our thorough attention to this distinction; *the basic concept [Grundbegriff] of philosophy,
the true infinite,* depends upon it."[90]

The limitation of the *infinite* by an opposed *finite*
must be removed by removing their independent and
opposed character and preserving them as interdepen-
dent elements in a higher category, which is—having
removed the opposition limiting the infinite—*the true
infinite.* In this process, the *independent reality* of both
the finite and the bad infinite, which is also finite, is
denied, and they are shown to be merely one-sided ab-

89. Ibid.
90. *Enc.,* sec. 95 (my italics).

stractions from a more concrete whole. Thus Hegel says that they are shown to be "something untrue, something *ideal*,"[91] and that "this ideality of the finite is the *main point* [*Hauptsatz*] *of philosophy*."[92]

It should now be clear that the need for a category which can adequately characterize the *infinite* reality of metaphysics is one of the major motivations of Hegel's *Logic* and its dialectical method.

PASSION IN THE LOGIC

Walter Kaufmann finds Josiah Royce's phrase "logic of passion" to be a felicitous expression for the spirit of the dialectic in the *Phenomenology*. Kaufmann has in mind the *Phenomenology*'s passionate attempt to push each form of consciousness, each world view, as far as possible, finally exhausting it and revealing its errors and limitations. He says, "Goethe was not only close to the spirit of the dialectic of the *Phenomenology* but probably influenced it profoundly when he wrote in his great *Bildungsroman*, *Wilhelm Meister*: 'Not to keep from error is the duty of the educator of men, but to guide the erring one, even to let him swill his error out of full cups—that is the wisdom of teachers.' "[93]

It is true, as Kaufmann says, that Royce makes much the same point about the dialectic as a general method not limited to Hegel: "Without erring, and transcending our error, we, as sometimes suggested by the Socratic irony, simply cannot become wise. . . . Error is not a mere accident of the untrained intellect, but a

91. *Enc.*, sec. 95.
92. Ibid (my italics).
93. Kaufmann, p. 170.

necessary stage or feature or moment of the truth as it is in itself."[94] But Kaufmann fails to make clear that, when Royce uses the phrase "logic of passion" a few pages later, he does not use it to mean what Kaufmann does. For Kaufmann, the *Phenomenology's* dialectic is itself a passionate procedure—this logic of passion is a passionate logic. Royce, on the other hand, is merely claiming that our emotions or passions are often contradictory or dialectical; his idea of a logic of passion is merely a logic modeled upon the contradictory character of our passions.

Royce is trying to explain the genesis of the "so-called dialectical or antithetical method." He argues that interest in the correctness of such a method could not arise unless one "had cases of apparently dialectical or antithetical thinking before his mind," and also that "the idealists believed themselves to be in possession of such cases."[95] He cites the "rapid and contradictory changes of popular opinion and social action" of the age—for example, "the outcome of the Revolution [of 1789, which intended to secure individual freedom] was a military despotism"—as "the first class of *illustrations.*"[96] Then he cites our emotions as a second class of illustrations of contradiction: "Of course this obvious instance of the revolutionary tendencies awakened the reflections of our philosophers. But the instance did not stand alone. All the greater emotions are dialectical. The tragedies of the storm and stress period, and of the classical and romantic literature, are portrayals of this

94. Royce, p. 79.
95. Ibid.
96. Pp. 81–82 (my italics).

contradictory logic of passion. . . . The fascination and power of Byron are due to his *contradictions*. Because of the loftiness of his emotional demands upon life he finds only triviality and failure."[97]

Royce then contrasts the passions or "passive emotions" to the "active will" and asserts that the will *better* illustrates the dialectic: "It is easy to say that all such phenomena express precisely the unreasonableness of the emotions. But a closer view shows that this dialectical tendency belongs rather to the active will than to the mere emotions."[98]

Royce cites the passions or emotions only as one of several illustrations of contradiction and as one of several models for the dialectical method, in which contradiction is a crucial element.

In discussing the virtues of the dialectic, Royce, like Kaufmann, points to the pedagogical worth of embracing and then transcending erroneous views. But unlike Kaufmann, Royce does not insist that these views be *passionately* embraced in order to reveal their error. To use Goethe's words, Royce asserts that "not to keep from error is the duty of the educator of men," but neglects to mention that one should "swill his error out of full cups."[99]

Kaufmann says only that "logic of passion" is "a fine phrase" and "a very suggestive phrase." However, by not making clear that what the phrase suggests to him

97. Pp. 82–83 (my italics).
98. P. 83.
99. Royce actually cites Goethe's *Wilhelm Meister*, but only for its contradictions: "There is a glory in winning all by abandoning all. Wilhelm Meister, like Saul, sets out to seek asses and finds a Kingdom" (p. 83).

is not what Royce meant by it, he undermines the orig-inality of his own excellent suggestion that the *Phenom-enology* not only uses a logic modeled on passions (emo-tions) but is itself a passionate logic.

Unfortunately, while Kaufmann thinks it enlighten-ing to view the *Phenomenology* as a logic of passion, he fails to see passion in Hegel's *Logic*: "The dialectic of the *Logic* is somewhat different from the dialectic of the *Phenomenology*: one could not possibly call it a logic of passion."[100] I want to argue, however, that Hegel's *Logic* is a "logic of passion" in exactly that sense of the phrase suggested by Kaufmann.

In support of his position, Kaufmann cites Hegel: "The system of Logic is the realm of shadows, the world of simple essences [*Wesenheiten*], freed from all sen-suous concretion. . . . Here it pursues tasks remote from sensuous intuitions and aims, from feelings. . . ."[101] Kaufmann concludes:

> Hegel still confronts us as another Odysseus: in the *Phenomenology* we follow his Odyssey, the spirit's great voyage in search of a home where it might settle down; in the *Logic* we are asked to follow him into a realm of shadows. There we moved in a world where the passions had their place; here the passions are left behind. We are to contemplate Concepts and categories—and see them as one-sided abstractions and mere shadows that are not what they seem.[102]

Admittedly, the *Logic* deals with abstract concepts rather than passions or emotions. But the treatment of

100. Kaufmann, p. 194.
101. *Logic*, 1:41 (Kaufmann's translation, p. 194).
102. Kaufmann, p. 194.

abstract concepts in the *Logic* is like the treatment of concrete forms of consciousness in the *Phenomenology*, just in that respect which makes the dialectic of the *Phenomenology* a passionate procedure. The passion of the *Phenomenology* consists in its completely unreserved embracing of each form of consciousness in turn —in its attempt to find in each a completely adequate way of relating to the world. Similarly, the passion of the *Logic* consists in its attempt to find, in each abstract category considered, the basis of a complete cosmology, an entire metaphysics, an adequate "definition of the absolute." In both the *Phenomenology* and the *Logic*, the passion of Hegel's dialectic lies in its attempts to find in each successive category or form of consciousness the ultimate answer to ultimate problems.

APPENDIX

Contents of the
Phenomenology of the Spirit

Preface

Introduction

(CC) RELIGION

VII. Religion
   A. Natural religion
   B. Art-religion
   C. Revealed religion

(DD) ABSOLUTE KNOWLEDGE

VIII. Absolute knowledge

BIBLIOGRAPHY

Ayer, A. J. *The Problem of Knowledge.* Edinburgh and New York: Penguin Books Inc., 1956.

Ewing, A. C. *A Short Commentary on Kant's Critique of Pure Reason.* 2d ed. London: Methuen, and Chicago: University of Chicago Press, 1950. Paperback reprint, Chicago: Phoenix Books.

Findlay, John N. *Hegel: A Re-examination.* London and New York, 1958. Paperback reprint, New York: Collier.

Hegel, Georg Wilhelm Friedrich. *Enzyklopädie der philosophischen Wissenschaften im Grundriße* (1830). Edited by Friedhelm Nicolin and Otto Pöggeler. Hamburg: Felix Meiner, 1959. Translated by William Wallace, part 1 as *The Logic of Hegel* (2d rev. ed., Oxford, 1892), part 3 as *Hegel's Philosophy of Mind* (Oxford, 1894).

———. *Grundlinien der Philosophie des Rechts.* Edited by Johannes Hoffmeister. Hamburg: Felix Meiner, 1955. Translated by T. M. Knox as *Philosophy of Right* (Oxford, Oxford University Press, 1942).

———. *Hegels theologische Jugendschriften, nach den Handschriften der Kgl. Bibliothek in Berlin.* Edited by Herman Nohl. Tübingen: Verlag von J. C. B. Mohr, 1907. Translated by T. M. Knox as *Early Theological Writings,* with an introduction and fragments translated by Richard Kroner (Chicago: University of Chicago Press, 1948).

———. *Phänomenologie des Geistes.* Edited by Johannes Hoffmeister. Hamburg: Felix Meiner, 1952. Translated by J. B. Baillie as *The Phenomenology of Mind* (2 vols. London: George Allen & Unwin, and New York: Macmillan, 1910; 2d rev. ed., in one vol., ibid., 1931). Preface translated by Walter Kaufmann in *Hegel* (see below).

———. *Sämtliche Werke: Jubiläumsausgabe.* 20 vols. Edited by Hermann Glockner. Stuttgart: Fromann, 1927–30. Supplemented by a very useful 4-vol. *Hegel-Lexikon* (1935–39; 2d rev. ed. in 2 vols., 1957).

153

————— *Die Vernunft in der Geschichte*. Edited by Johannes Hoffmeister. Hamburg: Felix Meiner, 1955.

—————. *Wissenschaft der Logik*. Edited by Georg Lasson. 2 vols. Hamburg: Felix Meiner, 1923. Translated by W. H. Johnston and L. G. Struthers as *Science of Logic* (2 vols., London: George Allen and Unwin, 1929).

Hume, David. *Dialogues Concerning Natural Religion* (1779). New York: Hafner Publishing Company, 1948.

Kant, Immanuel. *Kritik der reinen Vernunft* (*Original-Ausgabe* A, 1781; B, 1787). Edited by Raymond Schmidt. Hamburg: Felix Meiner, 1930. Translated by Norman Kemp Smith as *Critique of Pure Reason* (1929; rev. ed., 1933; reprinted, London: Macmillan, and New York: St. Martin's, 1958).

—————. *Prolegomena zu einer jeden zukünftigen Metaphysik* (1783). Edited by Karl Vorländer. Leipzig: Felix Meiner, 1926. Translated by Lewis White Beck as *Prolegomena to Any Future Metaphysics* (New York: Library of Liberal Arts, 1950).

Kaufmann, Walter A. *From Shakespeare to Existentialism*. Boston: Beacon Press, 1959. See especially chaps. 7, 8, and 9, "The Hegel Myth and Its Method," "The Young Hegel and Religion," and "Hegel: Contribution and Calamity."

—————. *Hegel: Reinterpretation, Texts, and Commentary*. Garden City, N.Y.: Doubleday, 1965.

Khayyam, Omar. *The Rubaiyat*. Translated by Edward Fitzgerald, 1851. Reprinted, Garden City, N.Y.: Doubleday, 1952.

Kroner, Richard. *Von Kant bis Hegel*. 2 vols. Tübingen: Mohr, 1921.

Marcuse, Herbert. *Reason and Revolution: Hegel and the Rise of Social Theory*. Oxford, 1941. 2d ed., New York, 1955. Reprint, New York: Beacon Paperback, 1960.

McTaggart, J. M. E. M. *Studies in the Hegelian Dialectic*. Cambridge: At the University Press, 1896.

Mure, G. R. G. *An Introduction to Hegel*. Oxford: At the Clarendon Press, 1940.

Myers, Henry Alonzo. *The Spinoza-Hegel Paradox.* Ithaca: Cornell University Press, 1944.

Neurath, Otto. *Erkenntnis.* Leipzig: Felix Meiner, 1932.

Nietzsche, Friedrich. *The Portable Nietzsche.* Edited and translated by Walter Kaufmann. New York: Viking Press, 1954.

Quine, Willard Van Orman. *Methods of Logic.* New York: Holt, 1950.

————. *Word and Object.* Cambridge, Mass.: M.I.T. Press, 1960.

Reps, Paul, ed. *Zen Flesh, Zen Bones.* Garden City, N.Y.: Doubleday, 1961.

Royce, Josiah. *Lectures on Modern Idealism.* New Haven: Yale University Press, 1919. Paperback reprint, ibid., 1964.

Ryle, Gilbert. *The Concept of Mind.* New York: Barnes and Noble, 1949.

Sartre, Jean-Paul. *Being and Nothingness.* Translated by Hazel Barnes. New York: The Philosophical Library, 1956.

Spinoza, Baruch. *Ethics.* Translated by R. H. M. Elwes. New York: Dover Publications, 1951.

Stace, W. T. *The Philosophy of Hegel: A Systematic Exposition.* London, 1924. Paperback reprint, New York: Dover Publications, 1955.

Strawson, P. F. *Individuals: An Essay in Descriptive Metaphysics.* London: Methuen, 1959.

Ziff, Paul. *Semantic Analysis.* Ithaca, Cornell University Press, 1960.

INDEX

Absolute: absolute knowledge, 4, 5, 31, 71, 111; absolute objects, 111, 112, 136; absolute power, 132; absolute reality, 136, 138–41 passim, 145; absolute truth, 47–48, 54–55, 61; the Absolute, 47–48, 51–52, 111, 112, 127, 131 n. 55 137, 138, 141

Abstraction: from concrete whole, 134, 139, 145–46. Abstract character of all thought, 92; abstract character of Hegel's *Logic*, 149–50; abstract nature of the thing-in-itself, 77–78

Accident, 35, 86; and essence, 108–9

Action, 12, 26, 29–37 passim, 43, 45, 144. *See also* Theory and practice

Aesthetic evaluations, 86–87, 88

Antinomies, 121–24

Aristotle, 49

Arnauld, Antoine, 38

Art, 4, 7, 73, 88

Asceticism, 41–42

Aufheben, 134, 139, 143 n

Aurelius, Marcus, 29

Autonomy, 14, 20, 28–33 passim, 42–46, 74–75. *See also* Independence; Self-sufficiency

Ayer, A. J., 36 n, 57

Being, nothing, becoming, 80, 138–39, 141–42

Berkeley, George, 64 n

Buddhism, 40, 42

Byron, 148

Christianity, 40–42 passim, 141–46 passim

Concepts (*Begriffe*), 27, 77, 113, 128, 131 n. 57, 133, 149–50

Conceptual analysis, 54–55, 58, 84–85, 97, 132, 135–38, 140

Consciousness: forms of, 4, 6, 8 n, 10, 102, 150; sec. A of *Phenomenology*, 8–9, 27, 43; use of term in *Phenomenology*, 8 n

Contradiction, 4, 35, 116, 122, 123, 129–30, 147–48

Descartes: 62; Cartesian concept of mind, 78

Desire (*Begierde*), 12, 14, 15, 18, 20, 26

Dialectic, 16, 130, 134–35, 138–41 passim, 146–50

Dogmatism, 119, 120

Eleatics, 138

Empiricism, 32, 56 n, 62, 63, 102, 111

Epictetus, 29

Esotericism, 132–33

Essence: 90, 110, 123, 137, 149; and accident, 108–9

Ethics, 6, 7, 73; Kant's, 4, 141–46 passim; skeptical rejection of, 35–37; ethical evaluation, 86–87

External object or world: affecting it through action, 26; attempt to know it, 27; its negation by self-consciousness, 11–17 passim, 20, 22; as object of empirical knowledge, 32; skeptic's denial of, 34–36; stoic's independence of, 29